SEX FROM AAH TO ZIPPER

....

A Delightful Glossary of Love, Lust and Laughter

By Roger Libby, Ph.D.

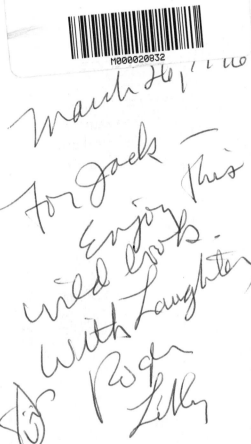

Illustrated by Julia Purvis

Cover Artist:
Salvatore Concialdi
Art Direction & Design:
Deborah Hill,
Online Creative, Inc.

Playful Pleasure Press℠ ©1993
Grand Rapids, Michigan

First published, March, 1993
Second printing, July, 1995

10 9 8 7 6 5 4 3 2

Manufactured in the United States of America

Library of Congress Cataloging-in-Publication Data
Libby, Roger W.
    Sex From Aah to Zipper
    1. Humor 2. Sexuality 3. Marriage 4. Relationships
    1. Title

Library of Congress Catalog Card #93-83088

ISBN 0-9635353-4-X

Playful Pleasure Press^{SM}
& GALLERIE EROTICA

P.O. Box 8733
Atlanta, GA 30306
(404) 377-5760
FAX (404) 377-6962

 ™ *The paper used in this book meets the minimum requirements of the
American National Standard for Information Services — Permanence of Paper
for Printed Library Materials, ANSIZ39.48-1984.*

 Printed on Acid–free, Recyled Paper

To The New Sexual Revolution

ACKNOWLEDGEMENTS

This book is the first of what will be a two–volume set. The second book will be titled **Hot Sex in the Cool '90's**. Playful Pleasure Press' next publication will be **The Pre–Sex Discussion (1996),** which will promote openness and honesty so potential lovers can make informed, caring and safe sexual choices. Our exciting new company will publish liberal and humorous pleasure books.

Sex from Aah to Zipper would not have been published had it not been for each of the following lusty, sensual souls: A. Morris, M.D., Al Dimmer, Gary Towers, Julia Purvis, attorneys Brad Shafer and Alan Nathanson, Mary Stafford, Kay Robberson and Richard Wroblewski. These key players contributed ideas, helped edit the manuscript and/or developed marketing strategies.

Gary Towers has added much to this book by editing and adding additional humor. His urbane sophistication and his fervent interest in sex complement my own liberal and uninhibited views. The text is equally enriched by Julia Purvis' hilarious illustrations. Julia is a delightful artist with a creative and truly funny flair. The sexy cover was created by Salvatore Concialdi, and the internal design was skillfully accomplished by Deborah Hill.

Many friends have contributed ideas for this book. Dr. Robert and Jane Pickett helped me focus my energy and my ideas. Dr. Jessie Potter made many helpful suggestions. Dr. Carol Cassell, author of the pioneering book **Swept Away**—which persuasively argues that women should enjoy sex without having to rationalize that they must first be in love—offered extensive comments on earlier drafts.

Dr. Ira Reiss and Harriet Reiss, authors of the insightful book, **An End to Shame: Shaping Our Next Sexual Revolution**, which takes a much needed rational approach to sex, have always kept me on the tips of my intellectual and emotional toes. The late Dr. Lester Kirkendall, my mentor in the sex education field, Dr. Albert Ellis, the Rev. Ron Mazur and Dr. Max Fitz–Gerald and Dr. Della Fitz–Gerald, all longtime friends and colleagues, inspired many of the thoughts in this book.

Additional humor, insights, marketing suggestions, editing and encouragement were offered by Lew Regenstein, who offered some of the funniest and most brilliant ideas, Ben Woodworth of Login Publisher's Consortium, Mike Malloy, Donna and Dick Gilmore, comedians Jerry Farber and Jeff Justice, Diane Pfeifer of Strawberry Patch Press, British illustrator Gray Jolliffe (famous for his Wicked Willie books), Bernadine Joselyn, Robert J. Sinclair and authors Marty Klein, Dr. Warren Farrell and Dr. Don Read.

To continue: John Kremer, Jan Nathan, Anne Barnes, Jacques deSpoelberch, Margaret Mortimer, Richard Simmons, Heather Hooper, Eunice Hess, Susan Rosmarin, Jeannine Addams, Shabori Red Bird, Cindy Husson, Dr. Jacqueline Boles, Dr. Ron Farrell, Chip Simone, Dan Liss, Carol Radzik, Dee Howren, Tina Caldwell, Johnna Lopez, Bruce Watson, Randy Ehman, Dave Livolsi, David Walker, Gwen King, Frank K. Graham and sexual activists Barry Lynn, Angela Faith, Will Jarvis, Paul Miller, Bill Baird and Randy Lee Payton of Rock Out Censorship.

Finally, I thank my parents, Marian and Don Libby and my brother, Dick Libby and his partner, Betsy Hartley, all of Seattle, and each of my playful friends and lovers for supporting my eccentricities so I could create my sexual art. My erotic vision will become a widespread reality as soon as we responsibly act on more of our wild and passionate fantasies.

INTRODUCTION

S–E–X! Hardly anyone has much good to say about sex anymore. We are witnessing a virtual epidemic of sexual piety and hypocrisy fueled by hyperbole about sexual dangers which is often a thinly–veiled attack on lust. In today's sexually sensitive moral, political and physical climate, how dare we openly discuss erotic passion in a humorous and liberal manner?

If you are a sexual enthusiast or sex buff—one who is cheerfully into celebrating erotic pleasure as often as possible—you must be tired of the abundance of sex–negative words. You must be weary of the notion that you're "promiscuous" because you enjoy two lovers, or because you've had sex with several.

We at Playful Pleasure Press are proud to introduce this witty, carnal compendium of sexual definitions. **Sex from Aah to Zipper** updates the tongue–in–cheek Glossary in James Thurber and E.B. White's classic 1929 illustrated humor book **Is Sex Necessary?** The clever, Thurber–like cartoons by Julia Purvis complement the text. From french kissing to self–pleasuring, garment groping, erotic massage, oral sex, intercourse and more, sex is viewed through a lighthearted lens. We need more pleasure–affirming words to visualize and affectionately express our sexual desires.

Noah Webster was in a position to be extremely influential through his choice of definitions for sexual words. Unfortunately, Webster was a true product of his repressive times, and he gave most sexual or sensuous words a very negative bias. This book uses Webster as a counterpoint for a fresh delineation of sexual matters.

Unlike the present author and illustrator, Webster spent so much time defining sex that he apparently failed to enjoy it. Since words are how we make sense of our sexual feelings and experiences, Webster's dictionaries from the early 1800's have made it difficult to be positive, healthy and humorous about sex. This book redefines and coins new words in light of today's sexual realities.

We anticipate a New Sexual Revolution by encouraging more playful and fully equalitarian erotic relationships. Sex can be safely and joyfully celebrated without guilt, sexually transmitted diseases (hereafter abbreviated as STDs) and exploitive games. Hey, it can even be FUN!

The double standard is discarded in favor of a single standard of sexual fun for both sexes. We heartily emphasize that wonderful F word. We treat women and men as equals, so that women are as free to initiate sex as men, and exploitive sex is not tolerated by either sex. Although sexual exclusivity is viewed as a rewarding and legitimate sexual choice for some, no assumption is made that monogamy suits everyone.

If there ever was a time to laugh about sex and immerse ourselves in orgasms, it is now. There is no rational basis for putting off orgasms until all STDs are conquered. **Sex From Aah to Zipper** is a contemporary sexual glossary that will help open up your eyes, mind and inhibitions.

Many media commentators criticize lust while extolling love, but the passionate combination of lust and love is rarely considered. Singles are often admonished to save sexual passion for marriage, or at least for monogamy. But there is no need to give in to unfair discrimination against sexual fun for single adults.

We are elated to offer **Sex From Aah to Zipper** as part of a conspiracy against those who would censor our orgasms. We can network with kindred spirits to promote more, better and safer sex if we use words which facilitate a happy outcome. Contrary to frothing-mouth moralists, there *is* such a thing as safe sex.

Nothing is 100% effective against STDs, but getting to know a prospective lover before having sex, talking about any concerns during a **Pre-Sex Discussion**, having both pre-tested for STDs, and using a condom and nonoxynol-9 are all **Safe Sex Steps** which greatly reduce the risk of STDs, unwanted pregnancies and hurt feelings.

To unleash our sexual potential we must reject rigid rules defined by stilted, anti-pleasure terms from religious fundamentalists and other extremists. The Puritans and Victorians were highly sexual in spite of severe repression. So are we, but we could be much more so!

Adding humor immediately spices up our sex lives! There is no reason to give in to doomsayers who shake their collective fingers at our playfulness. It's true that all STDs are not conquered, but we can control this risk. We won't be highly orgasmic unless we calculate sexual risks with common sense. We can responsibly limit risks without interfering with pleasure.

Let's get back to basics. Sex is fun, it's clean and it's healthy. It's not something to be ashamed and embarrassed about. There is no need to repress delicious sex. Sex is something to be enjoyed, relished, ravished and reveled in—a sheer delight!

Humor facilitates orgasms. We now know that Big O's are more than Cheerio Buffs on the loose at breakfast. As the French say, Vive la jouissance! (literally, "long live the pleasure to come!"). May you live long and come often!

Roger Libby, Ph.D.
Atlanta, Georgia
February, 1993

A

Aah: As in "open wide and say," this is the sensual sound of arousal, usually heard in conjunction with moans, groans and croaks (if you're a horny toad!), culminating with the screaming of your favorite deity. When used with proper inflection, pitch and volume, this word totally voids the need for anyone to ask "Was it good for you too?" Not to be confused with Aargh..., the sound emphatically uttered by a woman when a lover is laying on her hair. See Oooh, Mmmm and More.

Abstinence: The strangest of all sexual perversions, this is the sometimes voluntary but always frustrating avoidance of orgasms. Abstinence doesn't make the heart grow fonder, since the long–term practice of this form of self–denial is unnecessary, unhealthy, unnerving, unthinkable...well, you get the picture. Moralists who advocate abstinence ("Just Say No!") reveal their sex–negative attitudes—they never recommend masturbation, vibrators, outercourse or other sources of safe sexual enjoyment. Isn't it immoral to deny mentally and physically healthy pleasure to so many?

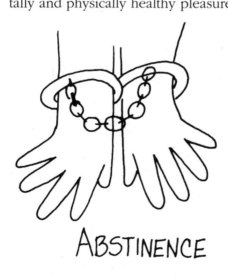

ABSTINENCE

1

Adultery: As implied in the root word, a favorite game of adults. Unrelated to archery except in the minds of aggrieved spouses. When a married person has sex with someone other than his/her partner, and the non–straying person is unaware or unhappy about the tryst. Although legal scholars, Webster and moralistic newspaper columnists don't agree, adultery does not include mutually consensual non–monogamous sex. Some husbands and wives do not expect sexual exclusivity for a lifetime. For some, extramarital sex is an entertaining and harmless diversion. See Swinging and Open Marriage.

Afterplay: A leisurely period of afterglow. Includes cuddling, soft kisses, dialogue and a feeling of relaxation and satisfaction from ecstatic playing around. You feel good from having done good. Does not include rolling over and going to sleep, or quickly putting clothes on and bolting out the door to a car with the motor left running. Webster doesn't mention the word, which implies that he missed out on one of the most intimate parts of sexual play. This omission is especially curious in light of his inclusion of aftershave and afterburner—concepts which seem related, if only abstractly. See Sexual Hangover.

Age of Consent: Your age the very first time you choose sex with others. When in doubt about the law, seek pleasure elsewhere. Sometimes it's hard to tell if a young girl is 14 or 18—but a jury knows the difference. Many people have gone to jail for their beliefs, but it would be a shame to go to jail because you *believed* your lover was 18, 16 or 14, depending on which state you became aroused in. See Teenage Sex.

Ageist: A person who prefers sex with a much younger person—entirely acceptable as long as the younger lover is driving age or older. There is nothing wrong with youthful lovers: taut young bodies are a turn–on, but older lovers often make sex last longer. Sex is less frantic, but kinder, gentler and, yes, better. You can double your pleasure, double your fun. Why not savor hot sex with lovers of different ages? Variety is the spice of life! Sex, like wine, improves with age.

Alternative Lifestyle: Any sexual lifestyle other than reproductive monogamous marriage. This includes singles sex, those in open relationships and swingers (those who exchange lovers at safe–sex parties). The term is commonly misused to describe gays, lesbians and bisexuals—sexual orientations with a variety of lifestyles. Americans encourage diversity except where sex is concerned.

In America many succumb to frothing–mouth moralists because they are more concerned about what others think about their sex lives than they are about expanding their erotic adventures. The incredible pressure to be forever sexually exclusive begins in the teenage years, and continues throughout the middle and later years. This is especially sad when you consider that women outnumber men as we age.

Sharing men makes good sense for unattached women, and men are equally charged with the extra attention! Conversely, women have a greater capacity for orgasms than men, so it makes good sense for some highly–sexed women to have several men and/or women available as lovers after their primary lovers wilt or fall asleep.

Alternative Lovestyle: A term used in forever–wild California for those who wish to experiment. Attracts less criticism because love is in the label. Such a concept is foreign to fundamentalist fanatics who preach a religion of love only if it meets their narrow, sanitized, dispassionate definition of what is proper.

Amateur Lover: A naive soul who cannot find the G–Spot, but who wants to experiment and learn how to stimulate orgasms, preferably from one or more pros. There is nothing more gratifying than coaching and playing with a novice, and turning her/him into a real pro. Webster defined a pro as a "devotee" and "an admirer" of a given pastime, rather than a member of a profession. Many yearn to graduate from amateur to professional status so they can receive lucrative endorsements. See Professional Lover.

American Family Association (A.F.A.): Unrelated to the American Sunbathing Association, this is a harshly intolerant and strident national censorship organization obsessed with keeping explicit sex and even sexual innuendo out of our sight and our hearing in the name of "family values." Founded by Reverend Donald Wildmon—a self-appointed "wild man" guardian of sexual repression, the Tupelo, Miss. based A.F.A. is high in visibility and low in common sense.

Our government has not officially recognized the A.F.A. as an arm of the Justice Dept., but the lack of separation of church and state makes such a fiasco an unofficial reality. After all, it was the Justice Dept. that sponsored the ill–fated and laughable Meese Commission on Pornography! The great American writer, H.L. Mencken, may have had this type of group in mind when he described the "American booboisie" as "A segment of the population composed of uncultured, uneducated persons." What Wildmon is advocating is so unhealthy and dangerous that it's enough to gag the Roto–Rooter man!

Amoral: A lesson to be learned from those who speak from heartfelt experience. A moral to a story should include an insight into how others can relish playful pleasure without incurring the wrath of anti–sex conservatives.

For example: there was once a very lonely fundamentalist who was frustrated and unhappy until he met a woman who was also reclusive, fundamentally religious and sad. They fell in lust, had sex, left their churches and lived and loved happily ever after. Moral: love is good. It's that simple.

Amorous: No, this isn't a knight or something covered with Armor All, but rather a sex buff who is aroused by a mixture of love and lust at the slightest provocation. Even a wink or seductive eye contact turns on such a marvelous, sensuous, sensitive lover. See Flirtation and Eye–Fucking.

Amuse: To add humorous dialogue to bedtime stories (First lover: "'Harder! Higher! No, softer...lower!" Second lover: "Come again? Make up your mind!"). Amusing monologues are also popular as long as your lover is a good listener during sex. If she/he falls asleep during sex–with–dialogue, you need to work on your jokes, your strokes, or both.

Anal: An adjective describing rigid, retentive types—those who are obsessed with limiting the pleasure of others by imposing unhealthy rigidities in the name of normality, decency and propriety. Anal people need a fresh outlook on lust. Our advice to them? "Get a life!" Also, an alternative orifice for sexual stimulation for some (proceed with caution).

A New Lover: A lover with new tricks and treats to please your pleasure palate. May be a lover of years or minutes. It will soon be as acceptable to introduce a new lover as it now is to introduce an old friend, especially if she or he is "new and improved." In spite of moralistic attitudes fostered by the media, the church and just about everybody in power, a new lover does not imply the exclusion of an "old" lover.

Aphrodisiac: Whatever drives you over the uncontrollable brink to seismic orgasms. Marijuana and oysters facilitate pleasurable sex for some, but neither works for everyone. One man reported that after consuming a dozen oysters on a dinner date, only two of them actually worked. Nothing can substitute for pheromones that attract us like bees to honey, and imaginative fantasies that we choose to act on. The best aphrodisiac is two horny people attracted to each other, especially when they are in love! See Rooster Pills.

APHRODISIAC

Arousal: Excitement caused by erotic fantasies, fondling and heavy kissing. Should also occur with yourself, although it's a challenge to kiss yourself in places where it counts. Arousal is a delightfully natural feeling that proves that we are alive, vibrant and vital.

Arousal Detector: A portable meter that measures pupil dilation and/or vasocongestion of blood vessels. Police can use such detectors to identify drivers who should be parked rather than driving while aroused (D.W.A.). Men are asked to walk a straight line while reciting the alphabet—difficult to do with an erection! See Autoeroticism and D.W.A.

AROUSAL DETECTOR

Astroglide: Uplifting sexual magic while in the clouds with an angelic lover. Close your eyes and drift up to Sexual Heaven. Also, the brand name for a superb, long–lasting sexual lubricant. Beware, your lover may refuse to return your Astroglide if you break up with him/her. See Magic and Pleasure Plus.

Attraction: A state of arousal caused by pheromones, which are given off by magnetic people within each other's range of smell and sight. The building of arousal from a generalized state of horniness. Romantics claim love is responsible for such an attraction, but love just adds fuel to the fires of pure lust. Falling in lust often precedes falling in love, resulting in confusion and mislabeling of feelings. "Coming attractions" are just that—celebrate your animal wildness! See Chemistry and Pheromones.

Autoeroticism: Sex in a moving automobile—often when alone, sometimes with a lover—preferably in a Saab. Arousal detectors are now available so orgasms–in–motion won't result in a moving violation (such as following too close!). See Arousal Detector and D.W.A.

Available: Turned on men, sometimes with little regard for marital status, and wild women who are able to transcend the double standard designed to limit their sexual variety. A few carry placards such as "I'll work for sex" or other advertisements, but many are available if you show sincere interest, tact, humor and affection. For specific sexual interests, consult the "Positions Available" section in the classifieds. See Easy and Free Sex.

Awesome: Literally, something that fills one with awe. The burning of the Hindenburg, Long Dong Silver, languishing oral sex and off–the–chart orgasms from both lovemaking and self–pleasuring. Few things in life are truly awesome, but positive sexual energy gives you an intense high, a new exuberance and a sense of purpose that nothing else can match. See Double Angel Ankle Lock Position.

B

Babbling: The sounds made by both a brook and silly people during listless sex. The former is usually much more wet.

Bad: Good. Colloquialism used mostly by college students to describe the power of being skilled at sex. Good sex is bad; very good sex is "wicked good!" No wonder a grammatically correct sex glossary is needed!

Bankwalker: Long ago, when men were men and women liked them that way, there were two basic kinds of guys you'd find skinny dipping at the ole swimming hole: those who'd strip, get into the water and stay there; and those who'd strip and spend more time on the bank than in the water, proudly strutting their stuff. The latter types—and their impressive appendages—were referred to as bankwalkers, as in "He's a bankwalker," or "He's got a real bankwalker." It's really an old, ten dollar word for being well hung. Question: what's the name for the female equivalent? Flowery lips? Petals of desire?

Bare Sex: Sex without clothing. Also, sex without covering, as in a condom. (Be sure to at least use nonoxynol–9 unless you are certain of your lover's safety). Not to be confused with BEAR SEX, which is illegal in most states, not to mention a bit on the dangerous side.

Battle Between The Sexes: A series of totally unnecessary skirmishes caused by a lack of effective communication between women and men—mostly over who should be on top and over the role of oral sex in modern lovemaking. The Eternal Struggle, producing no winners and many losers, where victory is defeat, and the only triumphs—or trysts—come during truces in trysting places (your place or mine?).

To quote the great civil rights leader King (Rodney, not Martin Luther), "Can't we all get along?" Let's negotiate a "piece" treaty, and celebrate each other's differences instead of fighting over them. We can then refer to the "other sex," not the "opposite sex." For a peaceful and pleasurable solution, see Pleasure Team, Tryst and Cum laude.

BARE SEX   (Not to be confused with 'bear' sex)

Being Selective: Canvassing an entire room of singles at a dance or bar before locating the most attractive person in the room, and approaching that person with finesse. The rarely acknowledged, but reasonable fourth option to abstinence, monogamy and promiscuity. Being picky without being exclusive, with special attention paid to each lover's sexual credit rating.

Caveat For Men: This does not mean selecting the woman with the largest or firmest breasts—character, intelligence and personality are most important. Caveat for women: this does not mean selecting the man with the largest wallet or the most expensive car. The myth about blondes being dumb is totally unfounded, although they often make men act that way! **See Sexual Friend.**

Beer Goggles: A "5" looks like a "10" when you peer through these. When you have more than a couple, your arousal and orgasms suffer. Too much booze spoils sex for all involved. Some are unaware that sex has been limited or terminated, because they are smashed at the time. And remember, friends don't let friends beer goggle.

Big Bang Theory: Possible explanation for the mysterious annual Spring migration of millions of college students to southern coastal areas such as Daytona Beach for courtship, spawning and spontaneous wild sex. See National Orgasm Week.

Big Brother: Literally, a large penis. Also, an authoritarian figure who is obsessed with controlling orgasms. George Orwell's 1984 is amazingly descriptive of North America in the 1980's and 1990's.

Bikini Brief: A man's brief bikini with an inspection sticker where the penis resides. The sticker always says "Inspected by Marilyn." Many a sexual encounter has been delayed or terminated from an argument about who got there first. Marilyn must be a very active woman!

Bikini Condom: A latex female condom worn by a woman on a hot date. Such sexual preparation gives new meaning to the word "anticipation." Like a good Girl Scout, she believes in the motto "be prepared." See Female Condom and Sexual Preparation.

"The bikini condom? Oh, I think it'll be perfect for St. Barts."

PHARMACY

BIKINI CONDOM

B.J.: An abbreviated blow–job. See Blow Job.

Bi–Curious: A term used in personal ads, usually by women who fantasize about sex with other women, but have yet to act on their desires. Those who are fascinated by duality of any kind, especially sexual. They appear to dream about sex they have not yet tried. Men are sometimes bi–curious, but refuse to admit it—another form of the old double standard.

Bisexual: One who has sex twice a year. Or one who, wanting sex, buys it. For some this term implies being aroused by both sexes. Woody Allen points out that this condition doubles your chances for a date on Saturday night. There's a new bisexual doll called "G.I. Don't Know."

Bliss: A state achieved during sexual union, especially when accompanied by love and caring affection. Also, the state of mind of right–wing religious zealots, as in "ignorance is bliss." Can't each side enjoy its own bliss without censoring the other's pleasure?

Blow Job: An oxymoron if there ever was one, since it is neither blowing nor a job. It is, however, great "work" if you can get it! Refers to playful oral sex performed on a man—a fantasy of incredible stimulation shared by many: those who love to give oral sex to a man, and by men who cherish receiving it. Blow jobs are a non–fattening feast for the provider!

Blow Off: As in steam. In the sexual/dating world, this either refers to: 1. bringing a man to a volcanic ejaculation through a blow job, or 2. a cavalier and often insensitive dismissal of a potential or actual lover, usually with little or no explanation or sense of manners. The best way to avoid an unwanted suitor is to say, "No thank you," while showing your appreciation for the implied compliment of the proposition.

Blue Balls: Discomfort due to a male's sexual arousal without ejaculation. Such a condition can easily be remedied by masturbating. Warning: ice packs won't help! An entire town is named Blue Balls in Pennsylvania. Apparently, the Blue Balls youth were fed up with parents who did not advise them on how to relieve natural sexual tension.

Body Language: Non–verbal body postures, movements and eye contact that tell you whether to speak, advance or retreat. Some tips: if eyes are open, the person is awake; if their arms are open, you're going to get a hug; and if their legs begin to open, you may be in for a treat. Body language is international in flavor, which means you don't necessarily have to know the words in order to have a hot time. Put another way, a "come hither" look can result in your coming within any zip code on the planet.

B AND D (Bondage And Discipline): Usually a light, mutual form of play with silk scarves or other restraints during sex play. Are you fit to be tied? See the classic movie, "The Story of O," to find out. For more heavy duty control and pain, see S and M.

BRA
SNAPS

USERS MANUAL

Bra Snaps: Perplexing latches specifically designed to confuse horny men about to embark on erotic adventures of the flesh. Also, a new slang expression for a special type of snack food. Not to be confused with ginger snaps or honey snaps, these must be nibbled on delicately after being removed from their packaging. See Garment Groping.

Breakfast Nook: Sex the first thing in the morning, when a man's testosterone level and sex drive are highly elevated. Breakfast in bed is a great way to start any day. Think of it—nibbling, licking, tasting and smelling the juicy, sumptuous delights of nature. Mmmm. And when your food arrives, you've really worked up an appetite!

Bull Hog Grind Position: An exotic position of sexual intercourse with orbital motions that slowly come full circle. Accidentally discovered by Atlanta comedian Jerry Farber, this wild position is not for those who lack athletic agility and endurance. Best after doing pre–sex stretching exercises. Usually leads to either the Lolly Plop Flop—a slight variation also perfected by Farber—or the Double Angel Ankle Lock position, and a very sore back.

Buns: That supple, sumptuous, fleshy part of the male anatomy which seems to first catch a woman's sexual interest. Generally ignored by males, who remain fixated on penis size in spite of all disclaimers about its importance. Gay males seem to be the only ones to "get it" when it comes to the attractiveness of buns, though football players must be aware of the interest they provoke—even if they put on an innocent front (or back). It is a well known fact in all macho circles that women do not have "buns." The structure in question is referred to exclusively as her "ass" when mentioning the female posterior. We gently suggest that this is a bit crude. Men should develop the same taste for "buns" as the ladies, so that all members of the Pleasure Team are at least speaking the same language.

BUNS

Bush Talk: Conversing with your lover while performing cunnilingus on her. Much more sensual—and sweet (as in Sugarbush)—than pillow talk. Also, emphasizing a political point, as in "Read–my–lips—or even better—kiss them!"

Busybody: A body actively engaged in wild sex. Also, a frustrated voyeur who makes disparaging remarks about those with an active sex life. Both meanings keep a person very busy.

California: Known unofficially as the Granola State, because of the misperception that it's filled with fruits, flakes and nuts. But to informed, intelligent, hedonistic libertines, this is probably the best part of the country to fulfill your wildest sexual fantasies with aplomb. Next to Orgasm, California is the closest state to Ecstasy! See Orgasm.

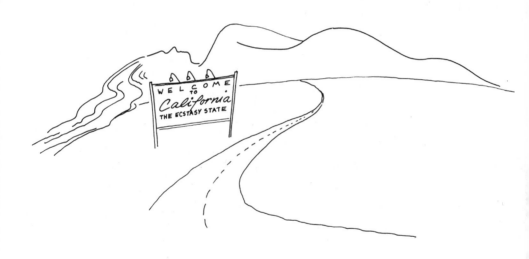

Californicate: To copulate in a variety of exotic and unusual positions. A person skilled at such fanciful practices is said to be a great lay.

Call In Well: To notify your office that you're not coming in so you can stay home and have sex to reduce work stress. Such a call should be welcome news to bosses who want happy employees, and who believe in sexual wellness as a part of good health. See Sex Break and Home Delivery.

Career Woman: A work–obsessed female who has sex–on–the–run: on the desk, on the plane, on the average several times a week, anywhere she can tastefully and discreetly get it. Involves home deliveries, airplanes, hotels and adventures on the road. Single career women are particularly imaginative in their quest for frolicsome adventure. When appropriate, they even have up–and–down sex in elevators. Career women deserve orgasmic relief from their stressful lives. See Sex at Work and Home Delivery.

Care For: When "I love you" is too frightening, try "I care for you" or "I'm fond of you." Caring, love and fondness are semantic nitpicking. You are either caring and loving or you aren't. When you say "I love you," it can be interpreted to mean you exclusively love that person—which may or may not be the case. For some, love and caring are like suntan lotions, the more they're spread around, the better they work. But for others love is a game of subtraction, where loving more than one detracts from both loves. See Love.

Casual Sex: Lust with a lover who is not turned on by monogamy or who enjoys being laid back (or laid in any other position) and erotic at the same time. Anti–choice moralists scream that anything short of monogamous sex is taboo, but sex buffs cheer for those who celebrate robust orgasms with like–minded souls. See Lite Sex.

C.A.T.: Short for the Coital Alignment Technique of intercourse where the man is above the woman at a tilted angle with his head to the left of hers, and where both lovers rock back and forth rather than thrusting. One variant on the missionary position which does not involve praying for orgasm. This is an extremely orgasmic posture for some women and their lovers. Others who try this position yearn to return to deep thrusting and wild gyrations.

Celibacy: An unhealthy practice and a bonafide perversion, this is abstinence from all sexual activity. Practiced today by some priests and nuns and a few friars during the middle ages. The opposite of celebrate—something the celibate rarely have occasion to do. Entered voluntarily by some, but often involuntarily imposed by repressed and insipid authority figures. See Abstinence.

Censorship: A sin and an obscenity in itself (sinsorship). This unfair practice is the misguided, unconstitutional and unhealthy effort to interfere with our private expressions of sexuality. A raging controversy over the attempt by government to control our lust–filled minds and our undulating bodies has invaded the bedrooms and parked cars of America.

The American Revolution, the fight for our constitutional freedoms, is not something which occurred in 1776 and is now over. It is a daily battle with those who would like to control our bodies and our most intimate expressions. Those who advocate and practice censorship should be glad that one early controversial book was not suppressed. The book features premarital and extramarital sex, homosexuality and masturbation. It's known as **The Bible**. See American Family Association, Christian Coalition and National Coalition Against Pornography.

Chaperone: One who is appointed, or feels compelled by social convention, to "protect" a young person—usually a female—from nonmarital touching and orgasms. In other words, when a chaperone comes with a girl, the latter usually doesn't. See Voyeur.

Chastity: Yes, this is the name of that tattooed singer's daughter, but a broader definition is abstinence from intercourse and, probably, all other orgasmic activity. Our advice is to use it before you lose it, because chaste makes waste. These are two thoughts that St. Augustine firmly understood, because he once said, "Oh Lord, give me chastity and continence, but not just now."

Chastity Belt: 1. A large, intoxicating drink we like to have whenever we think of the concept of chastity. 2. A region throughout every state where fornication–for–fun is frowned upon and preached against. 3. A centuries–old invention whereupon locked apparel covers one's genitals, with slots or holes which allow excretions to pass out, but no excited second party genitals to pass in. Chastity belts even curtail masturbation. For our money, anyone who makes someone unwillingly wear a chastity belt ought to be locked up.

Cheap Thrill: Sex without diseases and other problems that require doctor visits or other expenditures. Sex is a great show with no cover charge unless you are visiting a prostitute or someone seeking a "generous companion" in the personal ads. See Personal Ad and Sex.

Chemistry: A basic component of lust and love defying all logic, this is mutual attraction caused by raging pheromones and hormones and an overpowering and magical mix of all of our hungry senses. This chemical intoxication results in such bizarre and irrational behavior as dream–like trances, inattention to and easy distraction from work, loud singing, and even marriage. Great chemistry is as rare as steak tartare and should be celebrated just as passionately. See Pheromones and Magic.

Christian Coalition: The Reverend Pat Robertson's fundamentalist group hellbent on censoring any mention or depiction of earthly delights. A virtual Maniac Missionary Militia combating nonmarital orgasms, this large group gets a lot of sensational media coverage for its war against healthy sexual enthusiasm. For laughable details, see 700 Club.

Clean Sex: Good clean fun when both lovers have recently bathed or showered—preferably washing each other. Being squeaky clean can be a real turn–on, but only use unscented deodorants, and forget perfumes, as they cover up arousing natural smells.

Clitoris: This "joy button" for women is discreetly hidden amid the folds of the labia and operated by remote control from the brain. Once found, this delicate body part can be teased with tongues and massaged with hands to transform the human female into the greatest sexual athlete in the world. With the possible exception of the G–Spot in some women, nothing on earth compares to the orgasmic capacity focused in this tiny structure.

Many a drained and exhausted male will agree that the clitoris is probably responsible for the old Chinese saying: "Be careful of what you desire—you may get it." A good lover always provides plenty of clitoral stimulation. She will respond with total joy. For the male analogue, see Penis.

C.M.S.: Constant Moaning and Screaming during wild sex. The opposite of P.M.S.

Cock: A lusty term for a hard penis, usually near a woman who is wet with desire. When a man's penis is said to be cocked, it is ready to fire—and he is ready to crow. The term (and the subject) drips with virility, as implied in the derivations "cock–sure" and "cocky." See Lay and Rooster Pills.

Coitus Interruptus: Intercourse that is interrupted by an untimely knock on the door, a ringing phone, a burglar alarm, a cop with a flashlight, an annoyed neighbor or an angry parent. Also, the interruption of intercourse by an untimely withdrawal when someone else intrudes. A woman may levy a penalty for early withdrawal. She may also lower her rate of interest, or even close the account. Not recommended as a method of birth control, as it may result in a lengthy period of coitus interruptus due to an unplanned pregnancy.

Coitus Reservatus: Intercourse, often in a "no–tell" motel, where one or both lovers make reservations for sex at an hourly rate. Also, intercourse that does not result in a man's ejaculation until both lovers clearly signal they are ready. For some, this means having reservations about intercourse—such as it won't last beyond daybreak, it will result in genital soreness, or it will make you feel permanently bonded to a person you only want to excite occasionally. See Pheromones.

Cold Sex: Sex in cold places such as a walk–in refrigerator at a fast food restaurant during a sex break with friendly employees. Also, inserting a small ice cube in the vagina for heightened sensations during frenzied cunnilingus and ecstatically wild fucking. Caution: shivering can be mistaken for passion.

Come–On: What a man does to a woman's stomach after coitus interruptus. Also, orgasms on time (some use a timer!). But to many, the term means overt flirtation, sometimes with an approving audience. May be an actual proposition. See Hit On.

Comfort Zone: That area of your body where you enjoy being touched, licked, nibbled and otherwise stimulated. As your experience grows, so will your boundaries, until your immersion in orgasms makes you forget about any lines of sensual demarcation. Some offer new lovers an Erotic Map to alert them to their hot spots.

Coming Attractions: Future lovers with advance PR, including graphic sexual resumes with orgasmic details. See Pee Wee Herman Effect.

Coming Of Age: When youngsters have orgasms while passing through puberty and the age of consent—two rites of safe passage into the world of adult orgasms.

Coming Together: Formally called Simultaneous Orgasms, this is when two or more people climax at roughly the same time, but not always at the same place! Coming together should not be confused with coming apart, which is what happens to the minds of people who practice chastity. See Orgy and Phone Sex.

Commitment: Whatever we agree to do and not do. A ball and chain and clothing with black and white stripes often come to mind. A threatening word which inspires paranoia in those who cherish their freedom to be available for unexpected adventures. Traditionally, the Big C means monogamy, but commitment does not necessarily limit freedom.

Each monogamous partner may be viewed as continually free to choose monogamy. Those who wish to savor an occasional dalliance may still be committed to their primary partner. As pioneer sex educator Dr. Jessie Potter emphasizes, trust, fidelity and responsibility reside between our ears, not between our legs. Why should we feel compelled to define commitment by what we do with our genitals?

Sex means a lot of things in different relationships. We should be honest and keep or change our commitments. Enter freely into a commitment to enhance intimacy, but never succumb to an ultimatum! If your lover wants to be tied down, she/he may have scarves in mind—not possessiveness. It is unfortunate that commitment is commonly equated with limiting pleasure to one relationship. See Possessiveness and Pleasure Pact.

Compromise Between Women And Men: Leaving the toilet seat halfway down, and only hanging half your nylons on the shower rod. Given the different perceptions, needs and desires of the sexes, some compromise increases the odds for uncompromisingly terrific sex. Perhaps men could agree to stop teasing women about not being able to parallel park, write their names in the snow or pee in the shower. And women could stop getting on men's cases for not remembering their birthdays and ignoring them while sporting events are on T.V. A war between dumb blonde jokes and dumb men jokes is not a good compromise.

Condiment: Many fine hotels traditionally leave a mint on a guest's pillow. Modern hotels leave both a condom and a mint. Some leave a "condom–mint" as a way of saying "be sweet, be safe and have an orgasmic night." Also, any sauce a sex buff may use to spice things up. The cake may be the same, but the icing changes.

Condom: A latex sheath unrolled on an erect penis just prior to wild sex. An old but rapidly improving ingredient in safe sex, this wonder of pregnancy and disease prevention is constantly attacked by Maniac Missionaries who are obsessed with finding a way to stop our orgasms. Most condoms are marked "pre–tested"—good work if you can get it. See Pleasure Plus.

Condom Marshal: The local college dorm clown who frequently dances through the halls in a frivolous manner while distributing condoms to those who appear to be ready for hot sex. Sworn to confidentiality, such a person sometimes mutters to him/herself while receiving vicarious gratification from sexual activities. It's not a nine to five job. Beepers are essential—if your condoms aren't delivered within a half hour, they're free.

As the New Sexual Revolution begins, Condom Marshals will probably expand their services to include a broad range of sexual products. They may well become known as Safe Pleasure Marshals. Matt Dillon and Miss Kitty, where are you now that we need you? See Student Activities.

Condomnation: The successor to the Woodstock Nation, this is the generation of pleasure–loving people who refuse to forego orgasms because of an irrational fear of diseases—and who safely revel in lustful joy despite zealous and bitter condemnation from the Religious Right.

Condominium: Lowest price possible for a rubber. Also, an apartment bought or rented—frequently as a trysting place for her/his lovers. If you tryst in a condominium, keep every room stocked with condoms...then you'll have a condomaximum.

Conservative Republican: One who hypocritically claims to want to keep government out of his/her private life, but consistently makes exceptions when it comes to sex. Right–wing Republicans such as Pat Buchanan and Pat Robertson favor censorship of the mind and the body through a variety of laws designed to limit sex to reproductive marriage in the name of "family values."

Conservative Republicans appear to occasionally brave the pleasure of marital sex, but most of them don't frolic and immerse themselves in its wonder and awe. Such repressed politicos fail to celebrate orgasms enough to understand what it is they are so upset about others enjoying. Their sexually repressive policies give them the illusion of power and control over the masses. See Moderate Republican.

Contortionist: Anyone who tries the Double Angle Ankle Lock and/or the Bull Hog Grind position. Also, a typical conservative with a nose in everyone else's private lives.

Control Freak: One who must come up with every sexual maneuver without consulting her/his lovers. Such a person typically barks instructions designed to further personal pleasure. You can always sabotage this game by refusing to play by his/her rules. Share your fantasies so no one remains in control for long. Initiate with abandon.

Conventional Wisdom: The politically correct sexual philosophy popular at any point in time. In the early 1990's, this means you should avoid nonmarital sex, especially without a battery of STD tests, two condoms, a dental dam, a wet suit and a legal contract specifying damages in the event of any untoward outcome—such as an unwanted pregnancy, an STD or any negative feelings.

This isn't wisdom—it's paranoia. Pre–sex testing and

one of the two condoms is playing it safe, but paranoid abstinence and pleasure–phobia are terrible for your mental and physical health. Develop your own wisdom by being fully informed about your sexual choices, and have some sexual fun! See Sensible.

Coordinated Sex: Sex in sync, where no undue damage results. Where two or more hot bodies move as one, which helps keep you from falling off beds, high tables, ship decks, car hoods and roofs.

Cosmopolitan Woman: Inspired to a sexual frenzy by her favorite magazine, such a nymphet espouses multiple orgasms at the mere drop of her moist bikini panties. A modern, usually working, woman with a healthy acceptance of wild sex. See Playgirl.

Courtship: A combination of the "Love Boat" and "Divorce Court," where unhappy couples take a romantic cruise, get divorced and meet newly single lovers on–the–make. Also, that part of dating that focuses on future commitments more than present pleasures. Sexologist Dr. Albert Ellis refers to our dating customs as "sexually sabotaging." He is right. Romantic courtship should not end up in court. See Dating.

Couplitis: A severe irritation caused by an overbearing emphasis on being two rather than one. A fearful social disease. Singles are put down for not being half of a couple ("my other half"), because singles are often perceived as a threat to couples by one or both members. See Possessiveness, Hubby and My Wife.

Cover Charge: The price of a date if you are a man in North America. Unlike Sweden, where women pay their half, American women expect men to pay before they play. Conversely, men expect to play if they pay. A thoroughly artificial and often awkward arrangement where BOTH sexes overpay and underplay.

Crab: A frustrated person who is not having any luck clawing, grabbing, scamming, hooking up with, or otherwise locating a hot lover.

Cross–Dressing: Something that's a drag...literally. Dressing up in the clothes of the other sex. One who does this is also called a transvestite. Usually a man dressing up as a woman. Also, being pious while engaging in hypocritical sexual activities, as personified by Jimmy Swaggart and Jim Bakker, who appear to wear a cross while humping. This involves pretending to be something you're not, which implies sexual disguises, deception and hypocrisy. Blatant examples include the contrast between the teachings and the activities of many evangelists and catholic priests.

Cuddling: A warm, cozy interlude that occurs between lovers, often between orgasms. Unfortunately, many men would rather saw logs or quickly fall asleep than cuddle. Women can cure their intimacy problem with light conversation, light penis fondling, or both. Souls touch during truly intimate cuddling. See Afterplay.

Cultural Elite: A term used by conservative Republicans to describe Hollywood liberals, left–wing intellectuals, sexual progressives and anyone who can read and write. Conservatives lack any sophistication about sex. Inspired by envy, they are obsessed with sex because they aren't able to groove on it themselves.

Culture: A person's sexual preferences, particularly those aligned with a well–identified group or trend. Caution is advised for new travelers, as misunderstandings can arise. For example, someone asking if you enjoy Greek is probably not referring to baklava and shishkebab. Hurt feelings and difficulty sitting could occur, and you could be reprimanded for following too close.

Cum: This is an informal verb and noun—the former is great, and the latter is a wonderful masculine and sometimes salty reminder of the former. Some synonyms for the noun include ejaculate, spooey, jizzum, load and wad. Can also be spelled come, but cum seems sexier. Remember: what goes around can cum around, so use protection when in doubt about a lover being disease–free. See Orgasm.

Cum Laude: Screaming and other primitive sounds while in the throes of lose–your–head orgasms. Also, graduating with sexual honors. Easy cum, easy go. See Student Activities.

Cunnilingus: Oral sex (tongue–in–cheeks) with a woman. Involves the artistic use of a wicked tongue and succulent lips while licking and sucking an eager clitoris. Became wildly popular in the 1960's and 1970's. May eventually replace the goodnight kiss, although it's difficult to be private about this flavorful activity on a doorstep. Still illegal in several states with antiquated sex laws, but breaking the law never tasted so good! A man in Georgia was turned in by his lover for cunnilingus, and he was actually prosecuted for sodomy. And *you* think *your* technique needs improvement! See Fellatio and Go Down On.

D

Daisy Chain: Lovers line up with other lovers for simultaneous stimulation. Also, B and D (Bondage and Discipline) equipment for flower lovers.

Dalliance: A delightful alliance. Dillydallying with a lover rather than anxiously obsessing about the future of a relationship—and in lieu of reporting to work on time. Webster claims this means "foreplay," "frivolous

"Actually, my best moves are off the dance floor."

DANCING

action," and "amorous toying." What's amorous toying? Using a vibrator with love? See Lite Sex.

Dancing: Vertical foreplay, especially slow dancing. Put another way, one good Frug calls for you–know–what. Simulated and often sublimated sex, consisting of moving, gyrating and contorting one's body in harmony with one's partner to pulsating music. A mating ritual which sets the stage for orgasmic elation later on. The horizontal bop often follows the Frug. Prudes fervently try to ban rhythmic movements on the grounds that two should only tango behind closed doors, in the missionary position with the lights out, no doubt. See Horizontal Bop.

Dating: Planned social rendezvous between two (and sometimes more) people, ostensibly for fun, sex, a prelude to marriage or all or none of the above. Can lead to sex, but outdated dating customs discourage sex. Some women dangle sex like a carrot, while frustrated men try to figure out how to eat the carrot before possessiveness sets in like concrete. A date can be great fun, but exploitive games must first be firmly cast away. Then later, with any luck, pieces of clothing can flamboyantly be thrust away, to the delight of both. See Courtship.

Dating Etiquette: Archaic rules designed to delay or avoid sex. Such rules are concocted by those who have no earthly ideas. Indeed, dating can be a lot like playing poker: both bluff at first, then he sees that she has a nice pair, she thinks he has a good hand, and she raises him. Then he gets a straight. But unlike poker, both of these players win, even if one of them folds.

Delight: This is the thing you turn off when you want to do it in de dark. Also, it's a word that generally describes sex and/or orgasms, ecstatic experiences you can enjoy in de morning, de afternoon and de evening. Fantasies are powerful ways of reconnecting our minds and our emotions to our eager bodies. Make the connection! See Hedonism and Pleasure–Principle.

Democrat: One who is supposed to practice social and sexual equality. The double standard is strongly rejected in favor of egalitarian lust. In recent usage, this term is often synonymous (with emphasis on the sin) with "a candidate with a past." Some candidates are liberal and sensual enough to revel in their lovers, but lack the honesty to say so. This has the effect of making kiss–and–tell a national spectator sport at election time. It's a better bet than the lottery if your ex–beau is seeking office and you know a reporter for a tabloid. Tapes, notes and witnesses are usually needed to make the story credible. Most self–respecting Democrats bask in sex. For a more sorry lot, see Conservative Republican.

Desire: Lust with a focus. A powerful word conjuring fantasies of a specific person with raw sex appeal and a sexual resume that belongs in **Ripley's Believe it or Not**. Part of the mystical, mysterious, marvelous magic of romance and sex. Note: New Orleans is known as "The Big Easy," perhaps because it has a streetcar destination named "Desire," popularized in Tennessee Williams' play, "A Streetcar Named Desire." See Lust.

Dessert: The last course of a meal, usually sweet. Also, an extra orgasm or the final wave of multiple orgasms—which is always sweet. Try licking a hot fudge sundae with whipped cream off of each other's hungry bodies. See Evening Delight.

Differences Between The Sexes: Instead of opposites simply attracting and joyfully coupling, all too often this means "I'm OK, you're not." Men hate to admit they're lost, or to stop and ask for directions. That's why under Moses' leadership his people were lost in the wilderness for

forty years. Typical guy! Wouldn't admit he didn't know where he was. Women follow their intuition and their hearts, and some consult astrologists for advice about men. Men just follow women. Differences cause some of our sexual tension, as well as nonproductive conflict. A solution? Vive la différence!

Dirty: A term often used to describe sex which better describes the speaker. People who are dishonest about what sex means, and who manipulate others into sex. Some mistakenly use the term to refer to explicit and uninhibited sex, but as Woody Allen once said, sex is only dirty if it's done right. If "talk dirty to me" turns you on, be expressive!

There is much wisdom to the story of the guy who goes to a psychiatrist and is given a Rorschach test. Every time he is shown an ink blot he says he sees a couple having sex. Finally, the psychiatrist exclaims, "You really have a filthy mind." "Hey Doc," the man replied, "you're the one with all the dirty pictures."

Dirty Dancing: A couple engaged in good clean fun, such as the FBI twist, which is done undercover. To Southern Baptists, ALL dancing is dirty. To bonafide sex buffs, dancing is an erotic prelude to wild sex.

Divorce: "May divorce be with you" is something we never say, but sadly, divorce is all too common. Right now, about half of all American marriages end in divorce, which reinforces the new adage, "Love is grand, but divorce is twenty grand." On the positive side, many newly divorced people are among the horniest of all humans. A word of caution: rebound relationships can be more sexual than most, but recent emotional problems can often carry over to new lovers. Be careful to distinguish between being in lust and being in love.

Do: To "do" a person is to have sexual intercourse with him/her. On a college campus it's common to hear "I'd do him!" or "I'd do her!" Sometimes two people who feel this way are talking with each other—a done deal! "Do me" means just that. Do it!

Double Angel Ankle Lock Position: An athletic sexual posture requiring extreme agility and endurance. Not recommended for those who are out of shape or who lack coordination and imagination. A few lovers have had to be rushed to the Emergency Room with excruciating muscle cramps from staying in this challenging position more than ten minutes. See the Bull Hog Grind position—and see a good chiropractor.

Double Standard: The belief/attitude that there are two sets of sexual standards, one for men and one for women. The traditional double standard dictates that men can do anything they want sexually, but women—at least "good" women—should confine sex to one man at a time. This primitive kind of thinking has created monumental friction between the sexes, and it desperately needs to be amended. What's good for Jack should be equally fun for Jill. What the world really needs is a new E.R.A.—that's an Erotic Rights Amendment—giving men and women equal sexual rights, and that's why we've created one. See E.R.A.

Down Time: To a farmer, this can mean two things 1. The moment a goose is plucked, or, 2. The moment he and/or his lover is sucked. Ample down time is recommended for rewarding foreplay. When pants and panties are down, lovers go down on each other, genitals get wet and hard, and the temperature soars. See Fellatio and Cunnilingus.

Dry Humping: A Dry Run—or a Dress Rehearsal—rubbing against a lover without penetration, sometimes while fully clothed. Practiced by teenagers, dogs and single adults who are paranoid about unwanted pregnancies and diseases. Can result in genital soreness and stiff underwear. See Outercourse.

Dude: Complimentary term for a male who is popular with females. Can also be used as an exclamation: "Dude!", meaning "hello," "that's cool," "well done," "come here" or "why did you do that?" If said after a sexual interlude, can mean all of the above.

Dude Ranch: Resort where females vacation with the expectation of meeting and being totally satisfied by sexy, adventuresome, high energy males.

Duty: The expectation that one owes another a good lay. Sex should never be a duty—no one has the right to expect sex—but we all can hope for it! Also, a tariff on wild sex, usually punishment for pleasure from the law, religion or parents.

D.W.A.: Driving While Aroused. Fun, but can result in a ticket, accident, injury or death. Since you don't want to be prematurely going while you're cuming, we suggest pulling off the road when the pants start coming off. Masturbation and fucking while parked are two types of autoeroticism we favor. Sometimes stimulated by autoeroticism vibrators which plug into the cigarette lighter. To avoid traffic court, use discretion while courting in traffic. If you end up in traffic court, look around for a sexy person to meet, greet and treat! To a few, a love affair with a sexy car. See Autoeroticism and Arousal Detector.

DWA
(DRIVING WHILE AROUSED)

E

....

Easy: Whoever says yes to sex with utter ease. A normal person who desires sex without phony excuses. This term should always be viewed as a compliment, as it shows the individual loves sensual gratification. A true sexual enthusiast is only easy by choice. "Free" better describes such a healthy person than "Easy." See Available and Free Sex.

Ecstasy: The heights of erotic sensation, a sensual silent movie starring Hedy Lamar, or a popular love–enhancing drug...take your pick. We heartily recommend the first two, but the jury's still out on the latter. See Wild Sex.

English: Slang for sex involving leather underclothing, accessories, etc. The English are known to endorse a mixture of control and sexual expression. The confusion between pleasure and pain appears to begin in childhood, when parents and teachers use a ruler to hit the hands of an errant boy.

Environmental Lover: One who loves to make love in the woods, and under the covers with the lights out to save energy, or in tents, treehouses, canoes and on beaches. Also, women who use low–energy vibrators or call a friendly conservationist to drop by. Many are members of the Greenpiece and Save–the–Wails movements. Since sex is a renewable resource, is non–polluting, bio–degradable and doesn't harm the planet, let's all be sexual environmentalists. "Save the Planet—Have More Sex!" Join the birds and the bees—go for sex in the buff! Be the wild animal that you are!

E.R.A.: Erotic Rights Amendment. We hereby declare that all sexual acts should be equal, honest and sensitive. If a person opts for multiple partners, her/his lovers should have that option without strings or stigma—what's good for the gander shall also be good for the goose. Sex is a two–way street, and men and women should have and obey the same set of traffic rules, foremost of which is: treat others as you would have them treat you, and if it feels good for both lovers, it is good. As long as sexual responsibilities are balanced with sexual rights, celebrate sex openly, freely and frequently. It's way overdue for the E.R.A. to be happily ratified by everyone.

Erection: A description of what we experience when certain body parts swell after becoming engorged with surging blood. In men, it's the penis; in women, it's the clitoris; and in some special individuals, it's both! Sometimes confused with the evolution from four to two legs. Man has the largest (in relative terms) and most prominently displayed erection of all mammals. Perhaps nature is trying to tell us something! See Homo Erectus.

Erogenous Zone The skin. Especially genitals, nipples, the nape of the neck, ears and related areas. Women are said to have some eighty erogenous zones. Men are still trying to find them all. Men have one main one, and they know exactly where it is. But men also have others yet to be found by some women. Lovemaking should include a total exploration of each other's sensitive hot spots. See Y Intersection and Erotic Map.

Erotic: That which seems absurd and outrageous to all except the aroused individual, couple or more. Results in intense expansion of genital blood vessels. Stimulated by exotic fantasies, winsome smiles and rapid pupil dilation. This adjective simply describes a stimulus which results in arousal. Can vary widely, depending on culture, predilections, nationality, species and planet of origin. Unfortunately, this wonderful word has been misused in recent times to characterize only subtle or indirect images, and to exclude more literal and direct sexual portrayals which appeal to many. Both are, or can be, erotic. See Arousal.

Erotica: Sexually explicit materials that excite the user of the term. A speedy end–run around the socially unacceptable use of the term "pornography," this is a mutually arousing and elegant depiction of wanton desires. Touching, kissing, licking, sucking and fucking comprise much of erotica. In classy erotica, bicycle seats, high heels, crotchless panties and exquisite lingerie provide the basis for erotic fantasies in classy erotica. From the Greek word eros, which means love. Eros was the mythical God of Love, and his mother, Aphrodite, was the Goddess of Love. Erotica doesn't have to be exotica, but it often is. See Sex–With–Class.

Erotic Agent: A friend or hired professional who negotiates trysts by recommending lovers to each other. Friends do it for free, but may expect, as a vicarious commission, to watch early flirtation and fondling. Some erotic agents of both sexes also request the arousing details of the first tryst, thereby getting their own jollies. See Voyeur and Jollification.

Erotic Diary: Each person's compilation of her or his most memorable orgasmic escapades. Key lovers are given the accolades they deserve. The closest thing to an awards banquet is a juicy autobiographical book with real names, places and juicy details. Entrants eagerly look up their names in the index, compare their ratings with colleagues and rivals, and sign the book like a high school annual. See Sexual Resume.

Erotic Fortune: A fortune inserted in Chinese cookies. "Don't look now, but a new lover is nearby" is an erotic fortune. Warning: if an erotic fortune cookie results in sex, you may be hungry for it again in an hour. If you can't find fortunes in cookies, make up your own and insert them in a sexy person's pocketbook, wallet or bikini underpants. Your fortune may soon cum true!

Erotic Homeplay: Specific, goal–oriented but fun tasks assigned by sex therapists between sessions. Includes arousing each other, and then taking a sex break to discuss existentialism and Robert Rimmer's novel, **The Harrad Experiment**. Helps some couples improve their sex lives. For further information (and fees), see a certified sex therapist.

Erotic Map: A fantasy shared with a lover to guide a spontaneous adventure with no holds (or positions) barred. You can create your own erotic longitudes and latitudes enroute to oceans, rivers and mountains of orgasmic glee. What a trip! See Fantasy and Erogenous Zones.

Erotic Rolodex: A lay–away plan masquerading as a roll–a–way plan, this is a systematic accounting for a variety of potential and actual lovers. Includes local talent and long–distance prospects on easy–to–flip–over cards. Complete with brief comments on idiosyncrasies, preferences and fantasies of the lusty soul on the card. See Sexual Resume and Sexual Credit Bureau.

Erotomaniac: A sexual enthusiast with the time, interested lovers and energy to give and receive frequent orgasms. Also, a term used pejoratively to describe people who are sexually preoccupied with a particular person. Some therapists argue that erotomaniacs—particularly women with obsessive fantasies about men—are excessive or unreasonable in their sexual desires, and this is true if the obsession actually leads to invasive or violent acts. However, a few well–meaning professionals sometimes confuse strong sexual needs with personality disorders.

This unfortunate term is open to misuse by those who mistakenly think sex is too available. It is critical to remember that it is good and healthy to be enthusiastic about sex. Although this is obvious, we are constantly taught the opposite. See Sex Maniac and Sex–Crazed.

Evening Delight: Passionate sex with or without a light dinner. Often preceded by "We're staying in tonight—or at least HE is" (a long intromission). One couple got so carried away at dinner with the candlelight and romantic music, that between the main course and dessert they undressed each other and made love on the floor by their table. They literally feasted on each other, but they may never be able to get a reservation at that restaurant again! See Home Delivery and Dessert.

Exhibitionist Support Group: Where NOT sticking out is a measure of success. Self–help group for men who, when their wives remind them to drop their pants at the cleaners, rush over to do just that. Similar groups offer encouragement to women who wish to go bare–breasted in public, as out of the sunroof of a car. It all depends on what you are sticking out, and where you are at the time.

Some sick and perverted men who "flash" unwilling women and children have given exhibitionism a bad name. But pride in displaying the human body at nude beaches and selected other areas can be healthy, liberating, self–fulfilling and very impressive.

Explicit Sex: A precise depiction of unabandoned lust. An honest, graphic portrayal of the most natural acts, shown without concealment or ambiguity. Spurned by repressed zealots, vivid sexual acts represented by words, photos and erotic art raise the spirit, and sometimes more! Also, a straightforward appreciation of sexy bodies with cum–now facial expressions. See Pornography and Erotica.

Extramarital Sex: A little extra spice on the side of the main course. The saying "Extra! Extra! Read all about it!" often refers to the lurid details of an extramarital affair. Unfortunately, most extramarital sex in North America is a breach of the marital contract to only do each other. Can be dangerous, so pick extra lovers carefully! See Fatal Attraction.

Extra–Relational Sex: Same as Extramarital, except marriage is not involved. Those who desire a little extra simply savor others on the side, or on their backs, stomachs, etc. Some sex maniacs would be happier if they found a way to be honest when away from their Main Squeeze, but to others, ignorance is bliss. If you want to have fewer longterm problems, always be honest with all of your lovers.

Extra–Sexual Perception (E.S.P.): Foreknowledge that one is going to have sex with another person without a word about sex being spoken. Science explains this phenomenon through pheromones, which create a strong mutual chemical reaction resulting in acute arousal.

Extra–Terrestrial Sex: Any sex that is "not of this Earth," meaning human genitals getting pushed or pulled beyond this planet's gravity. To date, there have been no reports of sexual activity among aloft astronauts, even though men and women have worked together on joint space shuttle missions. This may change now that married couples are going into the cosmos together, because *this* final frontier should be very tempting! Also, outer space is lonely and cold, and there is no way to avoid sex whenever one or more people are left to their own endeavors for any period of time. Sex has universal appeal. See U.F.O.'s.

Extremist Feminist: An angry woman who blames her unhappiness on men's natural interest in sex with women. Extremist feminists such as Andrea Dworkin and Catherine

MacKinnon attack most heterosexual expression—including explicit sex, sexiness and male sexual overtures. Such women are extremely vocal, making it appear that their anti–male diatribes are shared by more women than is the case. Extremists give feminism an undeserved bad name. See Feminist.

Eye–Fucking: An intense, seductive way to attract a person to your secret fantasies. Eyes meet with anxious anticipation for what is to come—which may be you! The eyes have it! See Body Language.

Eye–Opener: To a coffee drinker, it's an early cup of Columbian. To a sexual enthusiast, it's sex first thing in the morning—sometimes just before or after a cup of tea or coffee. It's coffee or tea and me. Cheers, and pass the Astroglide!

EXTRA - TERRESTRIAL SEX

F

Faithful: Having the faith and keeping it. Following through on any agreement with integrity. Before vowing to "be faithful," make sure you know what is meant by "faithful." May include an ironclad rule to exclude others sexually, but may also approve of occasional responsible sex with selective others. During most marriage ceremonies, couples promise to be faithful without analyzing what they are agreeing to. "Do only unto each other" can be taken in more than one way. Some men say they would never cheat on their wives because it's hard enough disappointing *one* woman.

Old Faithful is a hot springs geyser in Yosemite National Park that faithfully comes about three times every hour. We're envious! See Fidelity.

Faking Orgasm: Making someone think you came, when you're still going—or stopped. A totally unnecessary, dishonest, base, and problematic practice performed by both sexes. Women sometimes claim this is easier than feigning interest in football or tuning a car. Men who fake orgasms are usually in a hurry, they're exhausted, and sometimes they're alone at the time! We should never fake pleasure, as this cheats our lovers and/or ourselves. See Coitus Interruptus and Cold Sex.

Fallen Woman: A female who becomes brainwashed by pleasure–phobic fanatics and feels so guilty that she reforms herself, becomes "born again" and abandons lust and passion for religious zealotry. Also, an ecstatic woman who tumbles out of bed during orgasm.

Family Values: An ill–fated attempt to limit sex to a guilt–ridden, clandestine action rather than an open acknowledgment of eroticism. Used by conservative Republicans to put down those who enjoy sex. It remains a mystery how we can reproduce if sex is not deemed appropriate as a topic of conversation, let alone an activity to cherish. Without sex, there would be no families, much less family values. Sex is the most important family value of all.

Fantasy: The application of hope and imagination to sex. A precise dream about incredible sex ("And then he traced my entire body with his wicked tongue..."). An exotic, sensual scenario where one imagines what it would be like to experience an arousing adventure. A fantasy can be acted on when the moment is ripe with desire. Your dreams can cum true.

Virtually all of us imagine far–out sex, but few of us admit it, even to our most intimate lovers—much less act out our visions. When we share our dreams, they can be acted on with delight. Lovers should always be understanding and accepting of their partners' sexual thoughts, and should never make fun of them, no matter how strange, unusual or bizarre.

Here's a fun exercise to try with a lover: the next full moon at midnight, each of you imagine and describe a scenario you'd like to act on. Then use the fantasy as your Erotic Map for orgasms galore. See Erotic Map.

Fatal Attraction: A highly acclaimed but dangerously misleading movie that gives new meaning to the phrase, "I'm CRAZY about you." One should exercise caution when having an affair. But the fact remains that the most dangerous aspect of affairs is still the autoerotic drive to the rendezvous.

Fellatio: Sucking and licking a penis and testicles. Accompanied by a chorus of aahs, ooohs and mmmms. The root verb of this word is fellate, which is Latin for "to suck." But remember, never suck or get sucked in a Latin class—the only hard things Latin teachers like are declensions. See B.J.

Female Condom: A new condom carried, and sometimes worn, by an adventurous woman. Since the condom is inserted in the vagina, a woman can be open to impulsive sex as soon as she drops her wet panties. Consists of a polyurethane tube and a ring at both ends. The inner ring is inserted by the woman like a diaphragm, keeping the tube in the vagina, and the outer ring outside the labia.

As with most birth control, this method unfairly relies on women to be responsible for disease and pregnancy prevention. When will the male pill be available, and will women trust men with this responsibility? Time—possibly centuries, eons or millennia—will tell.

Female Superior Position: A posture of intercourse permitting the woman to be on top and in control. Some argue that women are superior in any position, but others limit any female superiority to the woman–on–top–on her–knees (and feet!) stance. Men last longer, and women often get excellent clitoral stimulation. See Double Angel Lock Position.

Feminine Mystique: That arcane, charming mystery surrounding women. Why do women at restaurants always go to the bathroom together? Is there a see–saw in there? Also, why do women wearing fake eyelashes, fake shoulders and fake breasts always say they're looking for a REAL MAN?

Feminist: One who believes in equality between the sexes and behaves accordingly. Most feminists are not hostile toward men—and most do not view themselves as helpless victims. Feminists appreciate and love men as long as they are sensitive and loving, rather than domineering and aggressive. Some men have resisted the women's movement, but men are beneficiaries of equality too—we can have more intimacy and better sex with true equality. See Extremist Feminist.

Field Play: Sexual experimentation in a field, often with a class or group present, but sometimes when alone. Either way, this is hands–on, learn–by–doing, in–the–buff frolicking— usually under the sun, but possibly under the moon and stars. Universities should offer credits for learning about stimulating erotic touch.

Fiveplay: More Foreplay. Most men would be much better lovers if they weren't so quick to satisfy themselves. Women need more time to get fully aroused and satisfied. So be a pal!

Fling: A sexual sport in which you toss out the emotional ballast of traditional commitment, and enjoy the giddy ride of your body and mind with another carefree individual. The fling was thought of exclusively as a men's event until the late 60's, when women began to compete with and even excel beyond men in the sport. Women had obviously been practicing it in secret all these years. Although part of the Sexual Olympics, it is impossible to train for, since it is, by definition, impetuous. Also, a wild sexual dance culminating in numerous orgasms. See Sexual Olympics and Horizontal Bop.

Flirtation: Flirtation is an artful approach, a smile which lingers and a subtle gesture which lets the "flirtee" know that he/she is attractive to the flirter. When done with sensitivity and humor, this is actually the sincerest form of flattery, and a joy to all involved. The opposite of sexual harassment, flirtation is a "sexual compliment." Done with elegance and good taste, it uplifts our activities with others.

This is a word seriously in danger of extinction, and currently held hostage by the Catherine MacKinnon/Andrea Dworkin feminist fringe who shaped the Equal Employment Opportunity Commission's overly broad and ambiguous legal definition of sexual harassment. Flirting is a perfectly natural act. All animals do it: birds sing, horses prance, dogs sniff—and humans flirt—and sniff (remember our pheromones?). When returned, flirting is the first step in the dance of life, often culminating in sexual ecstasy. See Sexual Harassment.

Flower Power: The incredibly arousing power of a flower with labia–like petals and an erect pistil penetrating the folds with graceful ease. The symbolism is truly awesome! Gives new meaning to the curious "flower child" waiting to be expressed in all of us. Check out the Playful Pleasure Press logo!

Fly Buttons: Minor barriers to spontaneous lust present in outer garments in the genital area. Also, connectors to attach to guidelines so lovers make it back to earth after orgasms. See Zipper.

Focus On The Family: An illegal sexual orientation. Also, an ill–fated but quite visible attempt to limit sex in the name of family values without mentioning sex to begin with. The term is used as the name for a large anti–sex right–wing group headed by James Dobson. Like other conservative groups, they oppose big government and state interference in our lives—except when it comes to the bedroom or the womb. Dobson's group is determined to censor sex for the rest of us. He should focus on his own family, and leave the rest of us alone.

Foreign Affair: Meeting your secret lover for a discreet rendezvous at the International House of Pancakes.

FOREIGN AFFAIR

Foreplay: No, this isn't a golfing quartet, but rather, the teasing, physical fine–tuning that happens before intercourse. The word "more" often precedes this popular activity. Includes erotic massage, petting and french kissing. Some include oral sex. Foreplay is for play!

For some men, pulling down the zipper is sufficient. For most women, a little more is required. It is best to plan several hours for dinner, dancing, soft music, low lights, flowers, wandering violinists, whispered promises, an elaborate boudoir and lengthy kissing before making love. Many women expect this treasured activity to last at least 45 minutes, but it's not clear if this time frame includes driving over to their place. See Dancing.

Forty: A sexual watershed where some worry about their continued attractiveness and the future of sex in a society that emphasizes youthfulness. Many can overcome the difficulty of turning forty if they engage in aerobic exercise, eat a healthy diet and ravish available throbbing bodies. Many men love sex after forty because they have more patience and endurance, and so do women!

Women often come, literally, into their sexual prime after forty. Rounder, 40–ish women can be more sexy, more attractive, more technically accomplished (such moves!) than their younger, thinner and less experienced counterparts. Teenagers, who think they have the patent on erotic intensity, refuse to believe that sex actually gets better with age. What a shame that youth is wasted on the young!

Fox: Colloquial term of admiration for an attractive, sexy woman. The similarity in sound to the common four–letter epithet for sexual intercourse is obvious. Men often exclaim "what a Fox" as they attempt to negotiate a right turn at a red light, or as they walk or drive into a telephone pole. For the male equivalent, see Hunk.

Frederick's Of Hollywood: When you consider the phenomenal success of this lingerie company in the business of selling sexual fantasies to sex–crazed Americans, no one can say sex doesn't sell big, or that men don't want women to be sexy. A sexy negligee and enticing crotchless panties will turn on most men, not to mention the women who wear them! See Victoria's Secret. For kinks, see Cross–Dressing.

Free Sex: There is no such thing as a free lunch, but there is free sex (or free love, if your prefer), whether at lunch, breakfast or dinner. As long as no one attaches expectations such as an exchange of money, sex is free. If you are responsible, you can enjoy sex for free (except for the price of contraceptives or other medical services). Throb away!

French: Slang for oral sex, fellatio and cunnilingus. One of our favorite "cultures."

French Kiss: Intertwined, friendly tongues. Accompanied by heavy breathing and nearby oxygen masks, the activity should be mandated by the U.S. Olympic Team for team spirit exercises. Promotes a thorough understanding and enjoyment of arousal. The French call this "French Kissing." And Italian men don't call it anything, because they don't do it. Italian foreplay is "Maria, I'm home."

Frothing Mouth: A hung–up prude who can't STAND it when anyone enjoys orgasms without apologies. The term is accurately applied to conservative Republicans, T.V. evangelists, moralistic busybodies and other fanatic groups full of perverts (those who preach abstinence and other sex–negative propaganda). Should not be confused with a man or woman who has just brought his/her lover to a tumultuous climax from succulent oral sex.

Fuck: Literally, Fornication Under Consent of the King. A frequently misused lusty word conjuring images of extremely pleasurable intercourse. It's the most lusty act for most men and women in spite of efforts by some to divert attention to less enthralling alternatives. Sometimes referred to as a "dirty word," but "hate," "racism," "hunger" and "murder" are dirty, not words referring to acts of love and sex.

There's nothing dirty about two aroused lovers craving uninhibited lust. It's clean, it's fun and it's a more–than–friendly act when mutual arousal passes the point of light banter. Andrea Dworkin, Catherine MacKinnon and a few other misguided, extremist feminists tried to eradicate this essential practice in the late 1980's and early 1990's, but their efforts petered out!

If the power of lust implied in "fuck" is used for mutual delight instead of exploitation or trying to put someone down, it can arouse a lover. Unfortunately, "fuck" is often misused as an expletive to attack another, as in "fuck you," which should be a COMPLIMENT rather than a disparaging assertion. "Get fucked!" should be a statement of love and caring instead of a hostile insult. Following the thinking of sexologist Dr. Albert Ellis, it would be more accurate to say "unfuck you" if you wanted to deny erotic jubilation to another. See Undulate.

Fuck On A Dime: A Hip Hop term used by youth, which is sometimes adopted by those in middle age who wish to appear younger. It means "to rapidly hop on and hop off without any commitment." Often a one–night stand without any emotional connection. If a dime is too small, try a silver dollar. Also, sex on a small area such as a cot or a beach blanket.

G

Garment Groping: Arousing fondling and petting under outer and inner shells of clothing, and the eventual removal of all garments to facilitate easy access to eager hot and wet sexual parts. See Petting.

Gay: Those who are turned on by members of their own sex. According to Webster, a gay person is "happily excited," "keenly alive and exuberant," and "given to social pleasures." He was correct—all people should be "gay." Good sex makes us gay and happy. Heterosexuals can be as gay as those who prefer same–sex lovers.

Gentleman Lover: Neither macho nor wimp, this is an adventurous man who loves a woman's orgasms as much as his own. Such a man never does sex for profit. He has a sense of class without looking down on another (unless he's on top at the time). If he's with an airline flight attendant, he always returns her to her original upright position. And if he's with a member of the Religious Right, he returns her to her original *uptight* position! See Sex–With–Class.

Get It: Women argue that men should "get it" when it comes to viewing the meaning of sex as they view it. And men argue that women should "get it" when it comes to imagining sex (usually explicit) as they see it. The problem is that neither SEX "gets it" when it comes to a high rate of orgasms together. We desperately need a conference between the sexes so we can get it together and increase happiness for all. Get it? See Battle Between the Sexes.

Get Off: What a woman eagerly anticipates when she gets it on. He often gets on and she gets off. Also called an "on and off" relationship. A man also gets off—sometimes much too early—thus lessening the chance that his lover will get off too. See Orgasm.

Go Down On: Lowering your head in order to give head. Oral sex—cunnilingus or fellatio. However, depending on the positioning of lovers, you could go up on as well as down on. You may even find yourselves on a similar plane, making oral sex comfortable and wonderful for both lovers, as in "69."

Going All The Way: A sexual home run. Usually indicates sexual intercourse, but oral sex buffs claim they qualify too. A single involves heavy petting to orgasm, a double indicates blissful dry humping, and a triple includes hand and mouth stimulation of key erotic parts to trigger one or more orgasms. See Fuck.

Going Dutch: Refers to a dating practice, where at the end of the evening, the couple undresses and covers each other with gourmet fudge ripple ice cream, and then licks each other off. Some use this term unimaginatively to refer to the dating custom in which each pays her/his own expenses for the evening.

G–Spot: A dime–sized but million dollar–feeling orgasmic area about two thirds up the front vaginal wall that can trigger powerful female orgasms. This in turn can help facilitate ecstatic male orgasms. Light palpation of the area with a finger or two, and with the penis during rear–entry intercourse, can result in a gushing ejaculation that gives the term "wet spot" real meaning!

G–Spot and clitoral stimulation can also occur with hands and oral sex simultaneously performed. Strong pubococcygeus (PC) muscles surrounding the vagina encourage G–Spot orgasms. The discovery of this powerful erogenous zone gives new meaning to the term "G–Men," or, "Gee whiz, that was great!" See Sex Muscle and Rear–Entry.

GOOD GIRLS

Good Girl: The opposite of "good–time girl," this is a frustrated female who avoids sex because she has been taught she is naughty and she should feel wrenching guilt if she dares to luxuriate in orgasms. A woman that men want to marry but not have sex with except to reproduce. These men (and women) are usually disappointed with marital sex. A more appropriate description of such a female is Repressed Woman. See Nice Gal.

Good Guy: A sensitive guy who is good in bed. Some unimaginative women have written books defining a "good guy" as any man who will do whatever a woman wants in the name of chivalry and manners. See Nice Guy.

Good Taste: The wonderful taste (and smell!) of natural juices during oral sex and french kissing. It is important to taste as well as smell, feel, look at and hear your lover's expression of pure pleasure. This is good taste—suck–you–lent enchantment at its tasty best ("Oh, I can just taste you!"). In Alaska it's known as Tasty Freeze. It's always fun to be with people with good taste!

Gourmet Sex: Several courses of every sexual act imaginable. Languishing decadence at its hedonistic best. Sometimes topped by fragrances and tastes so exquisite and exotic that words can't fully explicate a thorough use of all seven senses (including intuition and humor) during steamy adventures of the flesh. Goes well with a glass of vintage wine, especially one that is bold yet mischievous, and whimsical but not presumptuous.

Got'Cha: A hide and seek (or find and fuck) game where lovers chase each other—often in the nude—and have their way with each other during a state of child–like play and raucous laughter.

Grabbing: Scamming when one person is more assertive than the other. Sex results from the explicit overtures of the grabber toward the grabbee. May include an unwelcome physical advance, usually by men who were taught to pursue sex in a selfish manner with no desire for an ongoing relationship. See Scam.

Grace: A piety uttered before a meal, or after delightful sex. Also, the thoughtfulness and class one would hope for in a sexual relationship. Grace requires open, honest feelings. When staying at a hotel, always check with the front desk to be sure an hour of grace is available at check out time. You may still be praying for orgasms.

Gratuitous Sex: A logical impossibility. We always get something out of sex, especially when coupled with caring. Used by religious extremists to put down all sex outside of marriage. The same fundamentalists rarely condemn gratuitous violence that relentlessly bombards us from movies and from television shows. It's sex that really upsets them.

Greed: A sin that has nothing to do with sex unless sex is exploitive. As Mae West put it, "Too much of a good thing is... wonderful!"

Greek: Slang for anal sex. Another popular "culture" for sexual aficionados. Requires relaxation, patience, sensitivity and a thorough knowledge of one's partner. Exercise caution. See Safe Sex.

Group Sex: Sex at the group rate in a large hotel. Usually involves three or more lovers simultaneously entangled. For some, the more the merrier. Also, for the less adventurous, one who engages in self pleasuring with two or more erotic magazines in the vicinity.

H

Hall Of Fame: A museum of erotic distinction featuring celebrities in such categories as: Politicians (Gary Hart, Ted Kennedy, Bill Clinton and even George Bush), Entertainers (Madonna, Warren Beatty) and Porn Stars (Linda Lovelace, Marilyn Chambers, Harry Reems and Long Dong Silver). It's also where ex–lovers and current lovers are eulogized for their remarkable talents.

Every sex buff has a Hall of Fame in her/his mind, if not in a photo album. The Library of Congress should have a special section devoted to the sexual trysts of presidents and members of congress. See Sexual Resume and Sexual Credit Bureau.

Hall Of Shame: A special wing of the National Museum for Television Evangelists called Holy Hypocrisy Hall, where the Jim Bakker Award for best portrayal of sex within the Church is displayed. Jimmy Swaggart is prominently featured with a special Voyeurism Award for the sneakiest observance of the beauty of the female body. And these are only the televangelists who have been caught!

Hand Job: A penis being manually stimulated, preferably by a second party. A couple of rules of thumb (couldn't resist): use a lubricant—it will be greatly appreciated; and if you're doing it yourself, use both hands. It'll kind of feel like someone else is pulling your member. Some women are experts at simultaneous oral and hand stimulation—artful play in the name of a job. But if you're Driving While Aroused, be careful to stay in your lane! See D.W.A.

Hanky Panky: Nonmarital or other supposedly intolerable sex. Webster calls such sex "illicit," but his assertion is probably tempered by being caught by his wife in his kitchen, where he was smooching with a maid. Upon seeing this sight, Mrs. Webster exclaimed, "Why Noah, I'm surprised!" Noah immediately corrected her by replying, "No, no, my dear...*I'm* surprised, *you're* amazed." Most people, young and old, love hanky panky.

Happy Trail: Also known as Treasure Trail—the line of light hair leading from our navel to our genitals. Teasing tongues, hands and bodily movements keep the trail clear enroute to a picnic at the bush. Happy trails! See Bush Talk.

Hard–On: An erection. The opposite of a "soft–in," which is why a penis and vagina fit together so well. A lover can stimulate such a condition with eager hands and a ubiquitous mouth. Caused by an inflow of blood, a hard–on is nature's way of telling a guy it's time to fuck. The only bad thing about a normal hard–on is that it often hasn't culminated in an orgasm—which may result in an uncomfortable condition called blue balls. See Erection and Wet–On.

Heavy Breathing: Deep breathing from the abdomen makes sex more intense and long lasting. Some forget to breathe when the crescendo of vasocongestion builds during torrid sex—a big mistake. Always remember to breathe as robustly as you gyrate. Steamed windows are a wonderful symbol that your trysting place is well heated from pulsating arousal and orgasms. You can always catch your breath while cuddling between—or after—intense lovemaking. See Tantric Sex.

Hedonism: The state/practice of pursuing pleasure. From the Greek word for delight, as in Epicurean Delight. They have a word for everything, don't they? This is everything right about the mutual expression of primitive desires. The pursuit of pleasure and the avoidance of pain are fine and dandy as long as they don't inconvenience others. Webster correctly states that hedonism is "the doctrine that pleasure or happiness is the sole or chief good in life." Sounds good to us! See Pleasure–Principle.

Hen–Pecked: A fortunate man who finds a woman to nibble his cock. If he comes in her mouth, she won't cry "fowl." Also, a man who feels overwhelmed by a woman who makes demands before she will lick, suck and nibble his throbbing shaft. See Cock, Lay and Pecker Tracks.

Hickey: Lovers who eagerly suck the nape of the neck while kissing passionately sometimes leave a tell–tale reddish mark which tells the world you were out of control. Sometimes it pays to advertise, but not everyone wants the world to know about their private pleasures. Can cause embarrassment at the office. The best lovers sometimes give and get hickeys because unrestrained passion is the orgasmic ultimate. If the office has hangups, try leaving the hickey in a more discreet (and more imaginative) erogenous zone.

Highly Evolved: Those lovers who are sophisticated enough to emotionally grow like a gorgeous flower. Such self–actualized people are concurrently creative and sensitive because they consistently transcend mundane dependencies on others. In other words, they've got it together. See Flower Power and Jealousy.

Hip Hop: A youth culture language used in some rap music. Occasionally used by middle–aged people who wish they were still young. Don't we all? Hip Hop words tend to reflect a selfish orientation toward all gratifications, including sex. See Fuck–on–a Dime.

Hit On: What a man with a hard–on does when in the general vicinity of a sexy woman. Usually a rather strong come–on. Some women hit on men, but they usually do so with more finesse than many men. Flirting and sexual overtures are mutually exciting as long as both parties are charged with each other. See Come–on and Scoop.

Home Delivery: When a lover delivers her/his hot body to your home to ravish you with undulating, tantalizing sex. Deliveries are made at lunch or before or after work, and they should be accomplished within thirty minutes of an arousing phone call—or you get the next delivery for free. With a home delivery, anticipation becomes foreplay, and lovers can contemporaneously do lunch and each other. Home Deliveries are a superb way to schedule loving lust during a busy day without interferences from work or children. Milkmen laid the foundation for this exciting practice—as well as many lonely housewives. See Sex With Class.

Homo Erectus: An aroused gay man. Though the term "homo" is extremely politically incorrect, we couldn't resist the pun. More sexual tolerance is needed. Discrimination against gays reflects the insecurities of the offender, called a Homophobe (one who is prejudiced against those who are gay, lesbian or bisexual).

Hooking–Up: A college student term which means locating, attracting and sexually connecting with another sexy person—

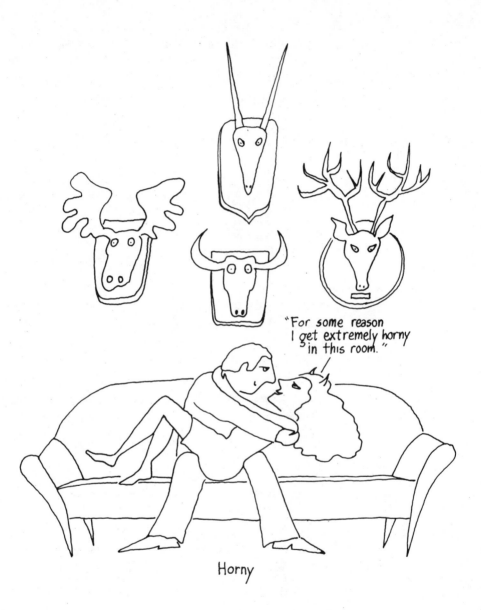

Horny

often in a bar or on campus. Can include "mugging" (succulent kissing). Today's college students rarely plan a date. Instead, they spontaneously hook up with kindred spirits, and then they have lite sex. Also, relatching a bra after sex play. See Scoop, Scope, Scam and Score.

Horizontal Bop: An orgasmic dance with a partner who shares your desire for rhythmic gyrations in unison. Often done to music, usually on a bed. See Dancing and Foreplay.

Horny: This means like or having horns. But since this isn't a book about antelopes, we prefer the definition "sexually aroused or lustful." Also, a person strongly motivated to celebrate orgasm(s)—usually with someone else. A horny soul has to settle for masturbation when an excited lover is nowhere to be found. For some, the word has a rather crude sound, so if it offends you, use the word randy. Hey, it works for the Queen! See Randy.

Horny Toad: A sex buff/enthusiast who identifies with a frog's glee while hopping to orgasms galore. We can all be horny toads searching for our prince or princess to turn us into incredible lovers. For official recognition and support for being a horny toad, join the National Organization of Sexual Enthusiasts (NOSE), celebrate National Orgasm Week (NOW) and patronize Playful Pleasure Press.

Hot Monogamy: A much preferred state over cold monogamy, this is a term used by some sex therapists to describe a passionate monogamous relationship—a fitting tribute to the power of romantic love and lustful imagination over stilted routines. Intimate fun replaces insipid habits in a vibrant monogamous partnership.

Hot Stuff On The Couch: An especially ravenous lover who is enthralled with heavy kissing and garment groping. Teenagers think they invented this practice, but their parents

"I'm beginning to understand why all our friends have become couch potatoes."

HOT STUFF ON THE COUCH

know otherwise. We can all be hot stuff if we turn off the T.V., and turn on the lust! See Garment Groping.

Hot Tub: A soothing, sensual experience where two or more lovers immerse themselves in a tub of flowing hot water while conversing about fateful encounters, love and romantic passion. Nudity isn't required, but it's definitely preferred.

House Of Ill–Repute: The U.S. House of Representatives, and the U.S. Senate, for that matter!

Hubby: A seemingly affectionate, but possessive–sounding term ("my hubby") bandied about by those whose only frame of reference is possessiveness. For the male equivalent, see My Wife.

Humpy: A horny yuppie; literally a Horny Upwardly Mobile Professional Yuppie. Often found in singles bars and driving foreign sports cars from countries we used to be at war with.

Hunk: Term used by women for a muscular, well–built, sexually attractive man who may or may not have anything upstairs. A perfect example of an unbalanced emphasis on physical qualities at the expense of the mind, because the latter stimulates the most provocative fantasies and ensuing sexual acts. And we used to think *men* had the patent on this type of thinking! For the female equivalent, see Fox.

Hustler: Usually a man On–the–Prowl, but also a woman looking for some action, sometimes (but by no means always) for money. The term generally has an aggressive connotation, but as long as the person being hustled is aroused, everyone should be blissful. Also, a tacky magazine.

I

Immoral: One who is dishonest or irresponsible about sex. Such a person may mislead potential or actual sexual partners about the true nature of her/his feelings and commitment. The term may also apply to one who is not sexually selective, and does not insist on a Pre–Sex Discussion and pre–STD testing, or at least the use of condoms and/or nonoxynol–9. Avoidance of these critical responsibilities endangers us all. Used misleadingly by moralists to criticize those who are more sexually active than they. The true height of immorality is when others try to make healthy, happy people feel guilty about sexual pleasure.

Incoherent: Public treatment of sexual matters by the U.S. Congress, the Supreme Court and the White House. Also, some lovers during wild sex. See Babbling.

Indecent: Whatever there is about sex that does not qualify as obscene. The U.S. Supreme Court, Congress and the FCC contend that explicit sex must be censored even if there is no logic to this imposition of prudish values. Prudery is hard to define, but you know it when you see it. Calling sex indecent is an illegitimate end–run around unconstitutional obscenity statutes encouraged by several senseless Supreme Court decisions. Curiously and sadly, sex is deemed indecent and obscene, while violence is met with social and legal numbness—this is what's obscene! See Obscene and Prurient.

Involuntary Abstinence: When you desire but can't find an appropriate lover who excites you. See Voluntary Abstinence.

J

Jealousy: The "green–eyed monster" described by Shakespeare, this is a negative emotion caused by an insecure person's fear of loss of affection. Basically, this means, "How dare you do that (have fun) without me!" Jealousy is an amber light warning that the relationship needs some attention. It can be controlled through heart–to–heart talks between affected parties, but it is difficult to eradicate. It's best not to talk about trysts with other lovers unless your main squeeze is extremely secure. Judging by their frantic and irrational behavior, extremist religious nuts are envious—a closely related emotion to jealousy—of the sex lives of sex buffs.

Jimmy Swaggart: A true–to–life televangelist who was unmasked as a bonafide sexual hypocrite. Swaggart preached hell and damnation while having a hell of a good time soliciting prostitutes. He is an unhealthy example of what happens when sex is repressed by fundamentalism. Amazingly, Swaggart's "sins" have been forgiven by some in his flock, and he continues to shear them! Others blindly follow other preachers who are better than Swaggart (so far) at hiding their clandestine sexual encounters.

Jollification: Holding your own. Celebration of orgasms with yourself. Masturbation or self–pleasuring. Especially appropriate during the holiday season—'tis the season to be jolly! Essential for a total appreciation of orgasms with others. Women especially need to cherish this wonderful tidbit by learning to jollificate at a young age—and thereafter! For men, an orgasm in the hand (or on a soft T–shirt) may not be better than an orgasm in the bush, but it's still damn good. See Self–Pleasuring and Masturbation.

Joy Button: The clitoris, which, along with the G–Spot, is a trigger for female orgasm. Every girl/woman should celebrate her joy button by stroking it appropriately, and by introducing it to her lovers. See Clitoris.

Joy Stick: The penis, especially when erect. Every boy/man should enjoy his penis and its propensity for enchanting stimulation to orgasm through self–pleasuring, hand and mouth stimulation and doing "the wild thang." Also, the control for four stereo speakers in a Mazda RX–7 sports car—a sexy car where there often is more than one joy stick to play with! See Wild Thang.

Justice Lover: The unabashed expression of erotic love for a fair judge, an honest lawyer or a friendly cop. Some Presbyterians include a sense of fairness, openness, honesty and caring in an erotic relationship. Both definitions show promise.

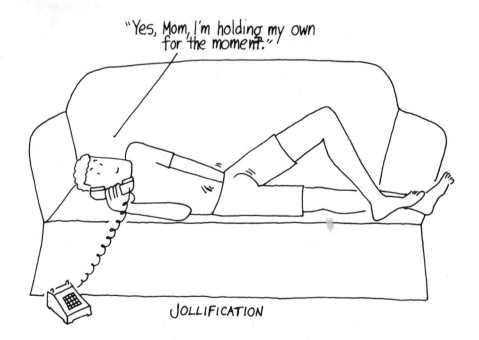

JOLLIFICATION

K

Kinder, Gentler Nation: What we will have when people start thinking about sex as something clean, healthy and wonderful, instead of dirty, dangerous and immoral. Will not occur with a Religious Right influenced government. Will we ever really have separation of church and state? The pursuit of sexual happiness depends on this separation.

Kissing: An intense sexual act distinguished by heavy breathing, lip and tongue action, licking and sucking and overall mouth–to–mouth and mouth–to–other–body–area stimulation. Prolonged kissing may require an oxygen mask, advance life support equipment, paramedics, nurses, doctors and healthy sexual friends. See French Kissing.

L

La Festa Di Lupercalia: A more uninhibited and erotic forerunner to today's Valentine's Day, this was a pagan fertility rite in Caesar's Rome about 55 B.C. when women chased men into the hills to have their way with them. Much less inhibited than a modern–day Sadie Hawkins Day, the men were dressed in lion skins and they ran like hell for awhile, but they eventually succumbed to the lusty women chasing them for a good lay.

Not surprisingly, Christians took the lust out of this day, and repressed Victorians in the 19th Century overemphasized romance, making Valentine's Day what it is today—a romantic day with little lust and lots of flowers. A man has to be a sexual athlete to make love with a woman perched on a pedestal—a very awkward position—especially when he is grasping roses with one hand! Perhaps this is where the term "a bed of roses" comes from, but roses are too thorny for the horny. See Valentine's Day and New Year's Eve.

Lascivious: Like "lusty," "licentious," "lewd" and "lecherous," this term connotes a preoccupation with sex. A lascivious person is one who uncontrollably drools over a tasty lover out of pure lust. Senator Jessie Helms has an attitude which says that lascivious behavior is a wanton indulgence in uncontrollable desires, but uninhibited humans don't care a twit about Helms and his ilk. Go with the flow of primitive desire! See Desire.

Lay: A noun and a verb, this is the quickest way to say "sexual intercourse" in the English language. Yet, quick is seldom desirable when it comes to making your own seventh heaven. From the word lie, this means to get someone or something horizontal, which is the easiest way to have sex. Just ask any missionary. "Now lay me down" has become a favorite bedtime story for those wanting more than a nap. See Hen–Pecked and Rooster Pills.

Laying In The Weeds: Patiently waiting for one or more sexy lovers to come along who show equal interest in you. Cruising without wheels, especially at the beach near the logs and tall green shoots. What anyone should do until someone who is truly appropriate and available comes along. The right person can come along at the wrong time, as when they are preoccupied with someone else. Timing is critical. When in doubt, don't!

Lecher: An older gentleman who yearns for young women's sexual charms. Unless the old man imposes his desires on a young woman, he is harmless. Some young women prefer sex with older men because they are more experienced than younger men, and they often last longer. The term is used disparagingly (as in "lecherous lout") to imply there is such a thing as getting too much of a good thing.

Less: A word not recognized by genuine sex maniacs. Frequency and quality of sex are both relevant to a great sex life. See More.

Lewd: Throwing dirt on sex to confuse those in the heat of the moment. Such rude behavior is typical of those who wish to oppress and repress others. Also, some use the term to describe lust without friendliness or love. Sex isn't lewd—it's fun! There is no need for negative sexual terms. See Repression.

Liberal: A generous, caring, open–minded sex buff whose Guiding Light is lots of responsible sex. Sharing pleasure and being kind to others are basic for a bonafide liberal. And what could be kinder than sharing your body with a friend. Sex can be your good deed for the day every day! A liberal's view on sex can best be described as "downloose"—the opposite of "up–tight." See Sex–With–Class.

Libertarian: A supporter of sex without a fee. Sometimes called free sex or free love. Also, one who supports, but may or may not practice, unrestricted wild sex. You usually get what you pay for, but since sex is priceless, it doesn't have a quantifiable value. See Wild Sex.

Libido: A person's sexual appetite (sex drive). Americans have a constitutional right to life, libido and the pursuit of happiness. Highly sexual people have their libido in overdrive nearly every day. Unfortunately, many peoples' libidos are in apparent hibernation. A first step toward increasing your libido is to engage in aerobic exercise and eat a healthy diet. A second step is to freely fantasize about whatever and whomever turns you on, and to use your arousing mental images during masturbation. A third step is to share your fantasies with someone who arouses you, and to act on them together.

Licentious: One who tosses sexual rules to the winds in favor of a good lay regardless of formal applications, a notary public or the ruling of a local judge. You don't need a license to be licentious. Consult an erotic attorney for advice on how to best deal with the Sex Police. See Lust.

Lipstick On The Collar: A sure sign of unrestrained passion from a woman with a bad aim. Other than a hickey, lipstick on a collar, face or neck is the most blatant tell–tale sign of lust—except perhaps for lipstick on a zipper.

Lite Sex: Fun sex without heaviness and rigid expectations or ulterior motives. Like Lite Beer, Lite Sex has fewer calories due to the absence of heaviness and/or obsessive sexual exclusivity. A pure delight where the emphasis is on present pleasure and humor rather than worry and tension. (such as "will I get it up?" and "will she come?"). See Casual Sex.

LOCAL TALENT

Local Talent: Lovers living nearby, usually within a short but arousing driving distance. Singles typically enjoy checking out local talent. More accessible than long–distance lovers who are G.U. (geographically undesirable).

Lonely At The Top: Feeling of despair by a man when there is no one at the bottom. Also, a similar feeling when a woman gyrates from the female–on–top position and the man fails to do his part. Those in power—especially repressed authority figures—often feel this way.

Lost Love: When one or both lovers lose interest in the other. You can go by the Lost and Found Department at the Sexual Credit Bureau, but when love is lost, it usually isn't found again with the same lover. There are exceptions—Melanie Griffith and Don Johnson, and Elizabeth Taylor and Richard Burton, for example. Yearning for a past love doesn't heal a broken heart. For a vibrant new lease on life, see A New Lover!

Love: The wonderful, energetic, exhilarating and sometimes painful feeling of strong attraction and affection of one person for another. Some say it's the ultimate positive emotion. Most agree it's the deepest form of enduring friendship. True love transforms the self into a greatly enriched and often more secure sense of being. Best enjoyed when reciprocated. Results in shared needs, goals and dreams. When you love someone, her/his needs are at least as important as your own. When this feeling is shared, life's greatest joys are ours.

There can be no passion without both love and lust. To experience love, we must rid ourselves of the fear of being physically close and emotionally vulnerable by trusting ourselves and our lovers to keep their commitments with us. This all sounds serious, but really, love is laughter, and love is a renewed vitality from feeling totally free with a cherished friend on an isolated beach or in the woods.

James Thurber and E.B. White refer to love as a "pleasant confusion," an accurate description of the sometimes irrational behavior which results. Since shared gratification is a goal, sex is the ultimate expression and reward of adult love, allowing bodies, minds and spirits to merge, mingle and maximize their affection.

Some who have experienced this transcendent feeling insist that a person can only love one other. But this is regularly disproved by those who love their parents, siblings, children and selected friends. Love simply grows as it includes more people. For some, this includes erotic love. For others, one lover is totally satisfying.

Being "in love" results in wild mood swings, erratic behavior, sudden outbursts of giggling and a restructuring of all priorities—not to mention an expanded awareness of who we are. Love would be considered a certified mental illness (passionate insanity) if its "victims" were not so happy and fulfilled. Arrows or not, Cupid makes us elated and complete. See Magic.

LUST

Lust: Positive, uninhibited arousal caused by wanton fantasies, fondling and lack of immediate gratification. Formerly viewed as sinful, robust lust is actually a virtue, providing the driving force for mutual love and joy. In youth, lust tends to be underrated because it is so plentiful, even if often unrequited.

Lust is put down until the golden years, when we wonder why we bought into the conservative "save it for" mythology. Waiting for pleasure is like waiting for Godot. Why wait? Life—and sex—will pass you by if you don't prioritize playful leisure. Who or what are you waiting for? Your body cannot be saved—it can only be enjoyed. Unlike greed and envy, healthy lust is not a sin. Neglecting it is a real shame!

M

Magic: Sexually speaking, this is when things go so well that they just can't be improved upon. Mutual ecstasy from a rare chemistry of sexual attraction while in the throes of love. Reserved for those lucky enough to find and explore each other without guilt, garbage and games, but with playful humor, soulful connectedness and heartfelt intuition. See Chemistry, Making Love and Passion.

Main Squeeze: The initial tightening of vaginal muscles on the penis upon entry during intercourse. Also, the most intimate lover who squeezes you (your primary relationship).

Make Out: The scintillating exchange of tongues, hands and moans, often while on a couch or in a parked car. The prelude to "making it." See Hot Stuff on the Couch, Aah, Oooh and Mmmm.

Making Love: A wonderful phrase, this is the creation of mutual passionate love where undulating bodies, free minds and open souls are synchronized. Intercourse, oral sex, kissing and fondling are the conduit for exquisite pleasure and magical feelings. The outside world is irrelevant when sexual artists collaborate on their own pleasure palate. Masterpieces can be created while souls touch during rapturous lovemaking. See Love and Magic.

Manizer: The analogue of womanizer, this seldom–heard term refers to a highly sexual, non–monogamous female who smacks her lips over seducing a variety of comely men. In contrast to its male counterpart, the term does not

MAKE OUT

Sex From Aah . . .

appear to be pejorative, and it is usually complimentary. One of several words which offer an alternative to the double standard. If we can accept and indeed extol manizers, we will some day think of womanizers without the negative connotations of exploitation and selfishness. See Womanizer.

Marital Sex: The first word is often confused with the word martial, which means war–like. For some unlucky couples, marital sex eventually erodes into martial arts. But some lucky couples manage to nurture their emotional and sexual feelings over a lifetime—the honeymoon never ends. They stay in great health, exercise, eat well and have lots of creative sex in plenty of different places at all hours.

Those with children should hire a sitter and head for a motel or a weekend away. They should also go to nudist parks and enjoy sex at lunch and at other unconventional times. Such couples savor passion into the golden years by constantly showing each other a new sexual wrinkle or two.

Marriage–Minded: One who constantly obsesses about getting married. Those whose primary goal (even before meeting someone) is to marry. Based on the often false premise that a spouse will do for you what you can't do for yourself: make you happy. Often self–defeating, since many a potential mate is scared off by obsession with commitment and the future. The following are sure signs of the Marriage–Minded: When she/he plans how many children you will have together before your first date. Is the reception catering arranged before you kiss goodnight the first time?

Masturbation: A word that sounds like something we should not do, masturbation is self–pleasuring, playing with yourself or jollification. The ultimate do–it–yourself hobby, it is enjoyed by millions, it is safer (and more fun) than bungee jumping, less time consuming than golf, and it's free! For the down–and–out, it's cheaper than dating, and you don't always have to look your best! More men masturbate than women—and at a younger age—but women are catching up! See Jollification, Self–Pleasuring and Autoeroticism.

MASTURBATION

Maybe: A word that makes absolutely no sense when it comes to sex. Is it yes or no? A thorough Pre–Sex Discussion should facilitate a mutual and definitive answer. No if's, and's or but's. See Yes and No.

Menopause: Men–who–pause to appreciate an older woman who continues to gracefully exude sexual desire.

Men's Liberation: When men no longer focus on their own gratification at the expense of a woman's orgasms. Like good wine, men usually become better lovers with time and experience. But rather than be gender–specific, we all need Sexual Liberation. See Women's Liberation.

Men's Movement: The movements men make during sex. Also, a social movement concerned with men's rites, and perhaps with maintaining male dominance for another few thousand years. No one is quite sure what this is or why it started, but many women believe it is one more excuse for men to go out together and beat–off—this time on drums! To be fair, some men in this movement favor true equality with women *and* close friendships with other men. See Women's Movement.

Mentionable: In North America, subjects containing violence, competition and aggression—behaviors which are rarely criticized by macho people and conservative Republicans. The same people blush and object strongly to any mention of sex—especially orgasms. See Unmentionable.

Me So Horny: Taken from the title of a popular album of rap music, this phrase has become the slogan, indeed the mating call, of an entire generation of young lovers.

Midnight Mass: The smooth, sticky and sweaty pile of bodies that builds up around the bewitching hour at a wild party. See Swinger.

Mile High Club: Membership composed of those who have had sex in an airplane or in Denver. May include the use of the restroom or available blankets while on the red eye special. Flight attendants often become extremely turned on when orgasms fill the air. Some masturbators have tried to join, but they have been told to start their own club.

MILE HIGH CLUB

Minutemen: Men—usually young—who experience premature ejaculation. Did Superman suffer from this affliction? He was "faster than a speeding bullet." Perhaps this is why he never married Lois Lane.

Miranda Rites: A formal ceremony where two lovers read each other a list of their rights, expectations, desires and responsibilities as they see them prior to a first sexual experience together. Occurs at the end of a proper Pre–Sex Discussion just before foreplay begins.

Such a sacred rite usually includes: "You have the right to remain silent...or you may graphically detail precisely which forms of sexual stimulation you prefer, how you would like them administered and the cadence that fits your mood at this moment." Some insist on an erotic attorney and a notarized Pre–Sex Contract, but this may be a bit laborious while in the heat of passion. It's more appropriate to honor an

MIRANDA

oral agreement with a deep french kiss, proceed to erotic massage and commence imaginative love making. See Pre–Sex Discussion.

Missionary: One who preaches the gospel of sexual joy and practices the doctrine of love and mutual hedonism for all. A zealous advocate who brings salvation from shame and converts the inhibited to join the ranks of the New Sexual Revolution. Total immersion baptism with such a high priest or priestess is highly recommended! Also, a popular sexual position which has been approved by the church only if nobody has too much fun. Some lovers pray for orgasms before entering the temple of desire. Such a prayer is also referred to as the "missionary position!" See Female Superior.

Mister Right: What women look for. Some settle for Mr. Right Now. See Ms. Right.

Mmmm: The sound of escalating arousal intertwined with aah and oooh, among other equally intense expressions of heavy breathing and stupendous orgasms. See More.

Moderate Republican: A Republican except when it comes to sexually punitive Republican platform statements about sex, sex education and birth control/abortion. Moderate and liberal Republicans are determined to pry all anti–sex planks from Republican platforms. See Conservative Republican.

Modern Lovers: Two or more highly evolved thrill–seekers who refuse to allow work, children or other interferences to affect frequent, passionate sex. Modern love is an art, and it should be regularly practiced by more people. A tip: try having sex in at least one new innovative place each week. Sadly, most people prioritize work and family responsibilities far above lovemaking. Is it any wonder that most people, as Thoreau wrote, "lead lives of quiet desperation?"

Monogamy: Traditionally, being married to one person at a time. An exquisite choice if both lovers continue to choose and embellish it with endless adventure, mystique and shared fantasies. Many Americans view themselves as monogamous when they limit all sex to one lover at a time, but this is serial monogamy, not lifetime monogamy. Monogamy can be agreed upon without duress, but it is sometimes entered without any discussion under the dubious assumption that both lovers actually agree to only do each other.

It is *love,* monogamous or not, that makes sex truly sublime! Most societies, including ours, are much less monogamous in actual behavior than in officially stated and politically correct policy, law and education. See Marital Sex and Responsible Non–monogamy.

Moral: The great English philosopher Jeremy Bentham defined this as "the greatest good for the greatest number." Since erotic enjoyment is truly universal, it is moral and healthy. More sexual activity and more numbers clearly constitute the moral life. A responsible and mutual sexuality is moral.

Morals: A set of rules governing personal behavior, under which sex is often considered immoral. However, any sex that is consensual, honest, non–exploitive, unselfish and mutually fulfilling is moral. By the same token, any undue lack of the above–described sex is immoral, as are those who advocate sexual deprivation.

Moral Majority: A misnomer. In truth, right–wing zealots compose the Immoral Minority. A fanatical religious group formed, disbanded and left in limbo by the Reverend Jerry Falwell to eradicate sex from the lives of those not joined by holy monogamy, and to ignore it for those who are so joined. Falwell, Ronald Reagan, George Bush, Pat Buchanan and Pat Robertson apparently copied the idea from George Orwell's 1984, where the Anti–Sex League was run by the government.

Resemblances between Congress, the Supreme Court, the White House, the Anti–Sex League and the Moral Majority are *not* purely coincidental.

More: Again and again and again. Always a good idea when it comes to sex, but most people never think of asking for another helping. Remember, sex is non–fattening, low in cholesterol and it is an exercise that truly does a body good.

Moresome: Those who wish to play with more than a twosome or threesome. More than a foursome is not allowed on most golf courses, but is more fun in a bed or hot tub anyway.

Multiple Orgasms: Bouncing with joy with several–to–many ecstatic bursts in a delicious row—a thrilling reward for being open to unabandoned pleasure with vulnerability. The ultimate in letting go, any woman (or man) is as happy as a clam at high tide as they cum over and over and over and. . .aah *yes!*

Ms. Right: A man's ideal woman—usually very sexy, hilarious and into sex as much as the horniest man. See Mister Right.

My Wife: Often used possessively to show that a husband owns his "little woman." For the female counterpart for a possessed husband, see Hubby.

N

Naked Pursuit: A very popular game which combines the idea of strip poker with any available board game. Those awarding points for questions, drawings, or guesses are best, but you are encouraged to be creative with any game! All you need is the game and two—or preferably more—adventurous adults with open minds, and romantic lighting. The rules are simple: Play the game as designed until someone wins a point. The person then gets to tell the person of her/his choice to remove a piece of clothing. The person who takes it off decides which piece to fling aside (drum roll...). Voila—Naked Pursuit, an intelligent, open–minded adult game whose results are anything but trivial!

National Chastity Association (N.C.A.): This forlorn group is opposed to premarital sex of any kind, including kissing, hand holding and falling in love before marriage (no kidding!). Members vow to wait until they marry to express their emotional and sexual feelings. True believers in chastity contend that sex will be better for the wait, but none is known to have attested to this after the fact. These unhealthy souls seek a rationale for their irrational and painful repression. This is fine as long as it is (1) somebody else, and (2) they don't claim moral superiority. See Chastity.

National Coalition Against Pornography (N.C.A.P.): Another frothing-mouth organization composed of sexually frustrated individuals whose apparent purpose is to make the rest of us equally miserable. This extremist group is well organized, well–funded, and a general nuisance and a threat to our constitutional right to be exposed to explicit depictions of orgasmic hanky panky.

National Organization Of Sexual Enthusiasts (NOSE): A group founded in 1990 by Dr. Roger Libby to promote caring sex and sex education, to fight censorship, and to combat "Just Say No" groups. Just say NOSE! Mutual hedonism and uninhibited lust are celebrated by both monogamous and non–monogamous members. Adds some much–needed humor to the debate over the role of sex in modern life, which heaven nose, we need more of! Publishes an entertaining and educational newsletter, *The Sexual Enthusiast.* For further information, send a Number 10 SASE to NOSE, P.O. Box 8733, Atlanta, GA 30306.

National Orgasm Week (NOW): The first week of Spring (third week of March) to start Spring with a bang! A modern–day Roman orgy created by Dr. Roger Libby in 1986 in Daytona Beach, Florida during Spring Break for horny college students who proudly wear pins that exclaim "I Came for National Orgasm Week!". And don't forget national Makeout Month and National Dalliance Day. Let's make every week National Orgasm Week.

Naughty: A nice person who gets passionately aroused and gets it on, especially in a place not usually devoted to sex. To savor a warm, eager body in any wickedly delicious manner or place. If you want to be naughty, try trysting in each of these adventurous places: in a park, in an elevator, restaurant, church, synagogue, closet, airplane, attic, basement, hot–air balloon (but not on the balloonist), hammock, train, shower, sauna, drive–in theater or eatery, golf course (where you're sure to get a hole in one), bar, swimming pool, pool table, tennis court, trampoline, cemetery, standing up, sitting down or on the floor. Wow! Naughty *and* nice are compatible terms. See Wicked.

Nervous: The feeling an insecure lover gets when she/he gets a busy signal while calling you from out of town. Also, the way you feel when you show up for dinner at a new

New Sexual Revolution: The third coming—the first occurred in 1929 and the second from 1973 to 1975. It is likely that the third coming will last even longer, and that it will spontaneously erupt about the year 2,000, or as soon as there is a vaccine for AIDS and the economy has rebounded. Its battle cry is responsible sex, and it's going to happen no matter what anti–sex bigots from the anti–porn New Left and the Religious New Right do to stop it. Shame will come to an end, and sex will be seen as a positive, life–affirming virtue.

New Year's Eve: The holiday most likely to turn into an orgy, beginning with those kisses at midnight. It's much more thrilling to have a New Year's Eve Sex Ball, rather than watch that one descend in Times Square. If you opt to ring in the New Year orgasmically, do it with a minimum of alcohol—the sex will be more pleasurable and long lasting, and New Year's Day will be less painful. See La Festa Di Lupercalia and Valentine's Day.

Nice: A sweet woman who denounces the idea that sex should be used as a carrot to wave at a man. Some believe the way to a man's heart is through his stomach, but a nice gal believes his genitals count too! She soundly rejects the notion that she must limit her sex life in order to be nice.

Nice Guy: It is said that "nice guys finish last." This should make them very popular in bed! A few boring female authors define a nice guy as a man who will do whatever women prefer, but a nice guy is just that—a nice guy. He is neither macho nor wimp. He is a gentleman lover. Women should encourage men to be more sensitive and thoughtful, and less tough and macho. This would benefit both sexes. Men especially need encouragement to overcome early socialization and society's pressure to be tough, strong and even mean. Some women feel nice guys lack sexual charisma. Ironically, this attitude can contribute to a woman's own exploitation. See Gentleman Lover and Good Guy.

"Now this, is a New Year's Eve ball."

NEW YEAR'S EVE

Sex From Aah . . .

Nicotine: An addictive drug delivered into the bloodstream by inhaling lethal fumes which lower arousal by tightening blood vessels and limiting vasocongestion of blood. Avoid nicotine if you want to be fully aroused. Every smoker asserts that he/she couldn't possibly handle more sex—a total rationalization to justify a deathly addiction.

No: An overused word. A favorite of anti–sex moralists to advise unmarried enthusiasts to "Just Say No" to sex. "No" has its place, but it's more proper to say "no thanks." Especially important for men: No always *means* no. But don't forget "yes" or "yes, please" when your juices flow for someone you are comfortable with! Equally relevant for women: Rather than responding to a man with either yes or no, why not *initiate* when you are interested? Just say "yes!" See Yes and Maybe.

Nymphomaniac: Defined by some as any woman who seems to enjoy sex. Literally, a woman who cannot be satisfied. Commonly and inaccurately used to describe a highly–sexed woman who prefers more than one or two lovers, or who experiences frequent orgasms. Moralists try to label any highly–sexed woman as a nymphomaniac in order to show that this is wrong, sick or perverted.

If the woman is able to reach orgasm and is satisfied by her activity, she is not a nymphomaniac—she simply enjoys sex! She often can be identified if the fire marshal closes down her bedroom for overcrowding, or by the presence of bleachers and cheerleaders in the bedroom. For the less used (because of the double standard) male analogue, see Satyr.

Obscene: Violence and the use of force, including sexual force. Explicit sex is called obscene or indecent without a shred of logic. According to our misguided Supreme Court, community standards are one criterion for deeming explicit sex to be obscene, but the Constitution and the Bill of Rights were never intended to be subjected to constant popularity votes by juries, Congress, state legislatures and public opinion polls.

In more healthy nations such as Holland and Sweden, violence is deemed obscene while explicit sex and nudity are appreciated. Unfortunately, in America if a movie shows a bare breast, it's rated R—but if someone shoots a person in the breast, it's rated PG–13. We think the latter is the true obscenity. The words sex and obscenity will someday be considered mutually exclusive. See Indecent and Prurient.

Obsession: Being in love. Also, a thorough drenching of the mind by lustful fantasies to trigger orgasmic explosions. If obsession with sex is a sin, let us all be guilty! Some lovers who break up continue to obsess about each other because of their magnetic chemistry. A few develop a "Fatal Attraction" whereby one of the two ex–lovers loses touch with reality for awhile. An even more sick and dangerous form of obsession is that found among sexually repressed Christian Coalition types, who are obsessed with the idea that somewhere, somehow, someone may be having a good time. Horrors! See Sex–Crazed and Pheromones.

On–The–Make: A horny person on the prowl for a kindred spirit—often in singles bars, health clubs and at a wild party. One of the most common On–the–Make stereotypes you might encounter is: "I wouldn't think of going home with someone I just met—until I have another drink." It's best to act with a clear mind. See Hooking Up.

One–Night Stand: A bedroom stand, usually wooden, with assorted sexual items—condoms, lubricants, vibrators, feathers, massage lotions and squirt guns. A Two–Night Stand is a bedroom equipped with two such stands. Some sex buffs decorate their bedroom/sexual playpen with assorted decadent night stands. Also, one night with a new lover that is not repeated—often a real shame! See the bedroom furniture and sheet sections of your local department store for examples of each.

Sales people who sell bed sheets have been known to demonstrate their sensuous qualities for the sake of ultimate customer satisfaction. Satin sheets are particularly arousing, but be sure that others are not in the area at the time. A back room with a lock is superb for brief trysts for those in need of a Sex Break. You could end up with one night stand, a set of sheets *and* a sexy demonstration that could be *repeated* during a Home Delivery after Calling In Well.

Oooh: A wild sound emitted when orgasm is imminent, contemplated, occurring, or just experienced. See Aah, Mmmm and More.

Open Marriage: This is where you love, honor, obey and sometimes play around. Unlike adultery, this is when both parties happily consent to equal freedom for both partners. The main squeeze receives most of a primary lover's attention. Extracurricular sex in an open marriage can occur with or without the spouse being present. The former is usually behavior more specifically defined as swinging. A sexually open marriage is one way for some who are liberated and secure to keep marital sex fresh and varied. See Responsible Non–monogamy.

Optimist: A sexual enthusiast who always carries condoms and nonoxynol–9.

Oral Sex: The Latin terms for this are *penis mouthus* and *clitus lickus.* Seriously, oral sex isn't something that should be taken lightly—it should just be taken and given as often as possible. This most intimate form of kissing is the most generous sexual gift lovers can give each other. A wonderful, sensual postscript to long hot baths or showers, oral sex is probably the single, sexiest form of foreplay you can enjoy. To some, it is the main act. Also, talking out of the side of one's mouth while licking and sucking clitorises and penises. A lucid conversation is difficult, but still possible. See Go Down On.

Orgasm(s): A wonderful genital sneeze that feels a lot better than the nasal variety. One or more peaks of desire taken to the max. The human orgasm is the homo sapiens equivalent of a pollen burst. What every person should shoot for every day and night. All that's required is one or more robust sexual organs.

An Epicurean Delight, orgasms are the highest and best pleasure known to human beings. Stimulated by fantasies in conjunction with clever hands, talented tongues, hungry mouths and relentless hip action. Lovers often moan and scream during this euphoric consciousness–raising state.

Is there anything more physically pleasant than an orgasm? We doubt it, as is amusedly exemplified by our female friend who recently visited her doctor. It seemed she was having an orgasm every time she sneezed. "Gosh," said her doctor, "what have you been doing to treat that?" "I've been sniffing a lot of black pepper," she gleefully reported.

Orgy: From the Greek word orgia, which means secret rites. Yes, orgies should be secret, and yes, we believe they're right for these reasons: they are fun, exciting, friendly, euphoric and honest. It is a real thrill to relish one–on–one passion in private, but it can be just as liberating to celebrate caring lust with a few close sexual friends.

If you're highly sexual, curious and secure, you might want to try an orgy with some safe, trusted sexual friends. There's no greater thing than love between two people—unless it's between three people, or four, or more! Odds are you'll come again and again. An orgy is a team event in the Sexual Olympics, with points being awarded for intensity, longevity and number of orgasms. See Wild Sex.

Outercourse: This has nothing to do with golf. Rather, it's a new form of pocket pool: rubbing against another sex buff to trigger orgasms without penile–vaginal penetration. Includes a variety of hand and body–to–body stimulation. Especially useful for teenagers, this is a form of safe sex not requiring the use of a condom. Nevertheless, it is still condemned by the Religious Right and those who believe any kind of premarital sex is evil.

The term "outercourse" originated in California where forever crazy enthusiasts are relentless in their search for safe sex. Californians will do anything to simultaneously (a) enjoy sex and (b) limit sex. See Dress Rehearsal and Dry Humping.

Overcome: To have too many orgasms. For genuine enthusiasts, there is no such thing! Also, to gag while giving a blow job. Note: the theme song for the New Sexual Revolution is "We Shall Overcome!"

P

Party Animal(s): College students and other socially and sexually gregarious souls who celebrate delicious flesh during or after a lively party. Also, a particularly friendly dog who loves to watch. Party animals have been known to do it from behind, on all fours, with and without leashes and, definitely, without inhibition or shame. Why should anyone be ashamed about celebrating animalistic, primitive and succulent sex? See Swinger.

Passion: The sweet and juicy fruit of mutual lust combined with love. Sex is best with intense chemistry and heartfelt love. As long as we band together as sexual enthusiasts, passion will always be in fashion—sheer ecstasy!

PC Muscle: Pubococcygeus Muscle in both sexes. Should be exercised regularly for more intense and more frequent orgasms. Not to be confused with being politically correct (selling your erotic soul to those who want to control you in the name of decency, love and appropriateness). See Sex Muscle.

Peccadillo: Spontaneous lust. Sometimes viewed as offensive or inappropriate, but there's nothing wrong with satisfying far–out fantasies with a hot lover. Not to be confused with a penile enhancer (a "pecker dildo") or a cross between a woodpecker and an armadillo. See Dalliance.

Pecker Tracks: Wet spots left in a hurry during an erotic hunt for the perfect orgasm. Marks on a man's pants (or nearby) caused by arousal. See Lay and Cock.

Pee–Wee Herman Effect: Embarrassment when others discover you get off in the dark. Also, taking your destiny into your own hands. Named after well–known television and movie star cuming soon in a theater near you. See Masturbation.

Penis: Pleasure–center for men. Operated by remote control from the brain, that powerful sex organ that makes a man hard or limp just by altering a fantasy or thought. In the case of some teenagers, the penis controls the brain. With all due respect to canines, it is the penis which is truly man's best friend. See Erection. For the female analogue, see Clitoris.

Penis Envy: A crazy "Freudulent" theory propounded as a fact by Sigmund Freud—who believed that women envy men for their penises. It's surprising that many psychotherapists still apply all of this hogwash in their therapy sessions! For a fee of course! For an opposing view, contact a representative of the American Association of Psychotherapists. See Vagina Envy.

Penis Size: North Americans are obsessed with penis size as proof that a man is a great lay. Length of the shaft is wrongly emphasized more than width—or girth—or net worth! Women with tight vaginal muscles (from doing PC exercises!) can relax, lubricate and jubilantly adapt to different penis sizes. See Sex Muscle.

Perfect Night: A sunset–to–sunrise delight where lovers focus their erotic and emotional energy on each other. Soft lights, rhythmic music, sensual massage, lingering kisses, caresses and lighthearted conversation contribute to a playful ambiance. Pheromones, candles, loving feelings and mental and spiritual connectedness make this a splendid night worth featuring in your Sexual Resume. See Erotic Diary.

Perfect Ten: Usually, a gorgeous woman. In the '90's, this is also a really sexy man. A perfect ten is also a four after you've had a six pack of beer, or a four with six million dollars.

Personal Ad: An ad for a date and/or a lover or mate. These ads typically focus on finding a mate rather than having a good time. Strangers demand that their soul mate be monogamous even before meeting them, and some ask for men who are "generous" (a man who will pay a gold digger for sex in one way or another). One example: "SWF, 32, seeks '92 BMW."

If women are overweight they say they are "full–figured" or "Rubenesque," and nearly every woman

PERSONAL ADS

wants someone who is financially "secure." Since age is a concern, people in their forties and beyond often don't list their age. Some ads are amazingly frank, e.g., "SWF seeks intimate and passionate relationship with a non–smoking SWM with large, expensive house and a late model foreign sports car to share. Serious inquiries only. Please send photo—of house and car."

If you place or answer an ad, be sure to meet in a public place, such as a restaurant. Some find dream lovers this way, while others encounter nightmares.

Pervert: A pervert is one who is unnaturally and zealously opposed to sexual pleasure for her/himself and for others. A prime example is one who abstains from sex for long periods of time.

Rabid religionists think this is anyone who gets her/his jollies by any means other than reproductive sexual intercourse. To the narrow–minded, this is any-one with sexual desires differing from their own. If you've ever masturbated, had oral sex, specialized in earlobes or navels, are gay or lesbian, or gone sexless for more than a few weeks, chances are you're a per-vert! But don't feel bad, because the New Sexual Revolution encourages responsible sexual experimen-tation. See Celibate.

Peter Pan: A man who prefers to keep the child in him as he ages. He is said by some to avoid growing up, but no such assumption is warranted unless the man is childish rather than child–like in his enthusiasm for earthy delights. It's never too late to have a happy child-hood! Also, a medical utensil found in hospital rooms.

Petting: Manual foreplay, something we applaud. Each generation of teenagers believes it invented deep breathing and heavy petting. We can envision Petting Zoos where aroused people meet, socialize and openly pet a variety of potential lovers before mutually assenting to vibrant oral sex and fucking. What a great idea—it sure beats eating popcorn while watching a gorilla scratch him/herself. Petting is, after all, a participant sport. See Garment Groping and Petting Zoo.

Petting Zoo: An arena where women and men fondle each other with mutuality, lots of flirtation, and fantasies of what is yet to cum. Voyeurs of all kinds love to watch. Heat is in the air, and perspiration cascades down the flushed skin of all involved. No admission fee is necessary, since this zoo is equally fun for petters and pettees. A day at the Petting Zoo is perfect for those who seek both variety and safety.

Pheromones: Extremely strong chemical substances which give off an irresistible and largely unconscious scent that spontaneously attracts particular animals—including human lovers—to each other. ("I have a nose for you!"). Those whose ravenous pheromones lock into each other usually don't resist acting on their highly charged arousal. We cannot control whose pheromones turn us on, but we can control what we do about our craving. If the person is not appropriate, we can simply leave the area. Or, we can listen to the chemical message and act on our desire for that person with unrestrained gusto.

There is such a thing as love at first sniff. This is one reason why we rarely feel sexy when we have a cold! Even our conscious sense of smell is a powerful attractant when the smell is just right. Using perfumes and scented deodorants covers up conscious and unconscious scents which would otherwise engulf us. See Chemistry and Attraction.

Phone Sex: When a conversation becomes highly sexual ("tell me exactly what you want!"), don't be surprised to hear moans and groans on Ma Bell's lines, usually followed by something like "thanks for the orgasm!" There is an erotic aura between lovers who are so in touch sexually that they can orgasm over the phone. Professionals charge for phone sex. Those 900 numbers where you can hear recorded conversations while masturbating are definitely safe sex—well...at least until you get the bill! When a wild married woman was asked whether she talked to her husband after sex, she replied "If there's phone in the room!" See Video Phone Sex.

"Thanks for the orgasm."

PHONE SEX

Play Around: A free–spirited sex fiend who plays house when around sexy people who attract her/him. Teasing, flirting and casual banter about the state of arousal, orgasms and innovative sex practices often lead to this hedonistic practice. Play makes sex mutual and fun. Webster was on target when he defined the term: "to behave in a playful or frivolous manner," but he blew it when he added: "to have promiscuous or adulterous sexual relations." Why can't we play around and be selective, sensitive, honest and responsible? See Sensible.

Playboy: A popular men's magazine also read by many open–minded women. Hugely successful from the beginning, *Playboy* has long been an institution, and Hugh M. Hefner, its visionary founder, has been visible and vocal as a symbol of the swinging good life. *Playboy Magazine* is said by some to be sexist and exploitive of women's bodies. There is no truth to this claim, except for the May, 1990 issue, "The Girls of Jimmy Swaggart." Liberal men and women read *Playboy* to stimulate sex and love in their lives.

It is not sexist or exploitive to be sexy—and to appreciate the other sex for its sex appeal. A playboy is said to be a guy who enjoys more than one lover, a fast car and other thrills. Uptight people refer to such a man as a womanizer. Philosophical question: how many private orgasms have been created in America with thy rod in thy right hand and thy *Playboy* in thy left?

Playful: A sexual enthusiast who celebrates pleasure with vulnerability and humor. Sex should be play, not work. All playful types understand and practice this...that's why they cum more, frown less and live longer. A tried and true aphorism: we do not stop playing because we grow old; we grow old because we stop playing. Sex is the ultimate intimate expression of adult play. Live, love, laugh and stay young.

Playgirl: A woman who enjoys more than one lover along with a fast car and other thrills. Uptight people refer to her as a whore, tramp, harlot and slut—unfair terms encouraged by the double standard, and motivated by envy and the puritan ethic that hates to see anyone else have a good time. We, however, resolutely salute playgirls, and we encourage them to see playboys and play ball as much as they like. Also, the name for a popular skin magazine intended for liberal women, but also read by gay men who like the explicit photos of men.

Pleasure Plus: An expanded sense of sensual delight experienced by those who are imaginative and brave enough to take a walk—or a roll—on the wild side. Also, the name for a condom that facilitates satisfaction more clearly and more safely than most condoms. The Pleasure Plus is the first condom with a new patented design in several years. The condom is looser fitting, thereby giving lovers the illusion that they are not using a condom. See More and Astroglide.

Pleasure Principle: The true "Peter Principle" that sexual jubilation is the top priority. A delightist's fantasy come true, this principle emphasizes numerous orgasms and wild thoughts galore.

Pleasure Team: A real dream team, this is two or more lovers who function together as a team devoted to mutual eroticism without exploitive games. Pleasure Team players pull and push together, and stay together much longer than non–team members. Being on the same Pleasure Team unites lovers against those who disapprove. Can help sustain a strong loving bond. May also include close friends and family who support and encourage passionate love.

Pleasure With Pride: Sex without shame, guilt or denial. See the New Sexual Revolution.

P.M.S.: Permissible Manslaughter. The reason women in the military would be good in combat, P.M.S. causes stress, anxiety depression and anger—and it's hard on women too. One argument against electing a woman President is that she might have to make critical decisions when she is cranky and unreasonable. So what if she acts like a man a few days a month? See C.M.S.

Polyfidelity: When extra–sex is agreed upon within a closed group of like–minded souls. Multiple fidelities among an orgasmic group who make and keep sexual agreements to only do each other. Variety and safety coexist peacefully with such a fun–filled arrangement. You can have your cake and eat it too. Conservatives frequently state that the only safe sex is lifelong mutual monogamy with a partner uninfected by any STD. Polyfidelity with an uninfected group of partners is equally safe, but mysteriously left out of the Surgeon General's report.

Pornography: Whatever moralists label as too sexy. Graphic sexual materials intended to arouse viewers. A term used to put down those who are aroused by sexually explicit portrayals in videos, movies and magazines. The root of "pornography" is two Greek words: "pornos" for "harlot," and "graphos" for "pictorial." Literally, it means "a harlot depicted." Under the literal definition, Biblical depictions of Rahab (who hid Joshua's spies in Jericho) and Mary Magdalene (who washed Jesus' feet) are pornographic. Jerry Falwell and Pat Robertson, where are you when we need you? See Erotica.

Possessiveness: The need, sometimes to the point of obsessiveness, to force someone to freely love you exclusively with total disregard for a lover's preferences. Ironically, expressing love in this insecure and selfish manner can negate, smother and kill the relationship. Total confusion exists between love and being possessive and needy in the name of love. Love is a gift from the heart, not a license to own a lover. See Jealousy, Couplitis, Hubby and My Wife.

POSSLQ: An acronym for Person of the Other Sex Sharing Living Quarters—which means you're living with someone who always hangs their laundry on the shower rod. You and your POSSLQ(s) may be same sex–lovers, boyfriend and girlfriend, occasional sex partners or just plain platonic roomies. POSSLQs provide all kinds of possibilities, especially as the number per household increases. You know what they say: two's company, three's a crowd, four's a quartet, and five or more is a possible orgy—or at least a Petting Zoo party. The U.S. Census needs positive, communicative terms for those in non–marital sexual relationships. See Orgy and Petting Zoo.

Pre–Sex Discussion (P.S.D.): The first step toward safe sex, this is a series of questions and discussions between two potential lovers before any decision is made about having sex. Common questions deal with contraception, the prevention of STDs, and with the identification of positions which can't be choreographed without a chiropractor's approval. Other questions concern honesty, openness, faking orgasms and whether each potential lover would be willing to trade off on who sleeps on the wet spot!

Some lovers are also careful to note any special desires for vibrators, kneepads (for whomever is on top!), feathers, massage lotions and squirt guns. Some require a Sexual Contract to avoid lawsuits from a spontaneous dalliance, but a thorough P.S.D. is an explicit Miranda Rite and more. Others are adamant about having a smoke detector and a fire extinguisher nearby (the flames from passion can burn up the best of intentions). It's usually best to conduct such a

PRE-SEX DISCUSSION

discussion before the fires of passion get too hot. See Miranda Rite.

Previous Life Regression: With the growing interest in reincarnation, more and more people are learning about their birth history through a process by which they experience their previous lives. It can be depressing, though. One poor soul learned that she hadn't been laid since the Civil War.

Professional Lover: One who is highly sensitive to her/his lover's preferences. A pro knows where and how to push all the right buttons and is highly practiced, but still treats each lover as special. A pro never falls into listless, boring routines. A diversity of paces of arousal and sexual positions, and a shift in conversation topics during sex are all appropriate. Take it from a pro if you can—you'll feel more sensations than you will with an amateur. But we all have to start somewhere. With consistent practice, you will soon be a professional, if you aren't already. And it's so much fun evolving into one. Professional lovers always do it for better—never worse—every time. See Amateur Lover.

Promiscuous: A sharp barb thrown at those with more lovers than the user of the term. Used to put down any sex beyond monogamy. One need not be promiscuous to selectively savor a few lovers. Usually, but not always, reserved for non–monogamous women because of the unfair (and weakening) double standard. See Slut, Tramp and Being Selective.

Prospecting: Checking out hot leads to locate and ravish lovers. Sometimes you do strike gold. A term used for traditional and mostly middle–aged men. These men would enjoy more sex if they got into the lingo of today's college student. But the dudes just can't seem to chill out. See Scope.

Prostate: The male gland which contributes to male ejaculation and orgasm. Sometimes confused with being prostrate, a state of being overcome. There is no such condition. We can never come too much. For the female analogue, see G–Spot. See also Overcome.

Prurient: The U.S. Supreme Court's infamous Miller v. California decision claims that if "the average person, applying contemporary community standards, finds that the work, taken as a whole, appeals to the prurient interest..," it is obscene. But the average person doesn't even know what "prurient" means! For the non–average person, "prurient" describes a delicious sensation of lustful arousal—a compliment to all who can evoke it. Since the word sounds a bit like "purr," we'd like to think that prurient sex fiends purr and make animalistic sounds of sheer pleasure as they play with each other. See Obscene.

Pubic Hair: Usually a small and triangular bearded area located directly over and on everybody's favorite body part. These hairs are delightful natural cushions for ardent strokes during animalistic sex, protecting the pubic bones of lovers while they bump and grind in unison. Many a lover has been known to compare pubic and head hair to determine if either has been dyed. But follicle thoughts soon turn to carnal ones, because the color of pubic hairs is of less interest than the succulent treasures they partially cover.

Purr: Combined with moans and primal screams, to purr is to be satisfied beyond words. Sounds made by cats only begin to resemble those expressed by fulfilled lovers during and after wild sex. See Prurient.

Pussy: A wildcat with curly short hair. Caress it orally and by hand, and it will purr.

Pussy Pie: An uninhibited and proud woman character created by the zany, irreverent British cartoonist Gray Jolliffe. For the male counterpart, see Wicked Willie.

Pussy–Whipped: Whipped cream on a woman's lower lips awaiting cunnilingus with a hungry lover with no apparent concern about calories or cholesterol. See Hen–Pecked.

Q

Quickie: Sex–on–the–run. A brief intromission—or intermission—depending on how you view the relationship between sex, work and children. See Home Delivery.

R

Randy: The British use this term to refer to horny people, but Americans tend to add in negative connotations such as being lecherous or crude. Americans have never fully accepted the generalized state of lustful desire. Despite the surface appearance of British reserve, England is far less repressed than North America. Randy is dandy. So is horny. See Horny.

Rear–Entry: For superb G–Spot stimulation, a woman can kneel over a bed or lean over a table to facilitate rear–entry vaginal intercourse. Called doggy style for obvious reasons. A nice variation for the true sexual artist. A natural for a secluded sex break in your office! One way you can watch erotic videos and have sex at the same time. See G-Spot.

Rejection: If you ask your lover to come to bed, and she/he says, "Right after the news is over," and she/he is watching CNN, you are probably being rejected.

Religion: Guilt with different holidays! Most religions label premarital and extramarital sex a sin. The Religious Right is so influential that some prostitutes offer a clergyman's discount. To be fair, a few liberal churches such as the Unitarian Church are sex–positive. See Jimmy Swaggart.

Responsible Non–monogamy: A marriage or dating relationship in which one or both lovers honestly, carefully and selectively feast on others as well as each other. Any extra–relational sex is celebrated with an explicit agreement between both parties. Some repressed folks believe there is no such thing as consensual non–monogamy, but they are wrong. Helps prevent monotony, and can add spice to a primary bond. Does not suit all, but some find their lives enriched by acting on their fantasies with more than one lover. See Being Selective.

Responsible Sex: Trustworthy sex with the light on, so you don't forget to play it safe. This is where the saying, "We'll leave the light on for you," comes from. Also, sex with openness, honesty and common sense. Marriage and/or monogamy aren't requirements. To be responsible and orgasmic, all we need to do is learn to tune in, turn on, drop our underwear and open our minds. See Safe Sex.

Resurrection: Rising to a second or subsequent sexual encounter within a short period of time with full blood flow and accompanying wetness and/or hardness. Also, new life for what may have been construed as a lifeless form.

Rita Rudner Effect: An attitude toward men on the part of some knowledgeable women of humorous contempt, good natured derision, subtle sexual liberalism and friendly satire. Not based on bias, bitterness or meanness, but on actual experience with men, and a resigned realization and acceptance of their faults and foibles. Such a gentle woman feels that sex should be cooperative rather than competitive. She is right! See Pleasure Team.

Romance: Making love, as opposed to just doing it. Romance in a sexual relationship is doing all those nice things to your partner that you would like done to yourself: sending flowers, cards, gifts; putting a big towel over that wet spot; gently bathing his/her genitals with a warm, moist washcloth after passionate sex. Just try to emulate a lustful Emily Post or Cary Grant, and you'll do fine. Also, putting women on a pedestal—a difficult position for mutually orgasmic sex. See Valentine's Day.

Rooster Pills: Pills with inert substances tauted as aphrodisiacs by those who imagine themselves as sex–crazed birds. Said to be good for cocks, but are really nothing to crow about. Also taken by women to increase desire. The placebo effect often makes lovers believe that the pills offer new sexual vigor. Available in some drug-stores and adult sex shops. See Aphrodisiac.

Run–On Sentence: Two or more words said together during sex. It's best not to use crib notes by the bed, semicolons, long declarative sentences or rhetorical questions during sex. Short sentences, even fragments, facilitate a virtual melt–down from having devoured each other.

Rush Effect: The effect of totally repressed and irrational people on the lack of a healthy approach to sex. Named after Rush Limbaugh, an outrageous, irrational, misinformed, pompous and unpleasantly plump talk radio show host in the early 1990's. Rush groupies prefer money and censorship to sex. His first name probably characterizes any sex he might have, although he appears not to have sex at all, preferring to blow off his energy and frustration into the microphone instead of a vagina or other orifice. Rush is popular because he is entertaining in his effort to tap into the shallow, unsophisticated, unhealthy and negative nature of other frightened and hostile North Americans. Some people actually take him *seriously!* See Frothing Mouth and Conservative Republican.

S

S And M: Sex and more. When someone says she/he is into this practice, they have ropes, chains, spankings and dominance and submission in mind. If you call someone who claims to be "tied up right now," consider taking them literally. Bondage and discipline (B and D) is a more playful version where lovers use scarves to take turns tying each other to a bed while acting on extremely arousing fantasies. See B and D.

Safe Sex: This used to mean doing it in a bank vault so nobody could catch you. Today, it means locking your car when you're parked, and locking your home doors, as well as avoiding those with potentially angry spouses or other jealous lovers, your boss (or employee) and anyone under the age of consent.

Seriously, given that there is some risk of sexually transmitted AIDS and a higher risk of other STDs, be certain to conduct a proper Pre–Sex Discussion and use nonoxynol–9 in a water–soluble lubricant or spermicide and/or a high quality latex condom.

There is no one formula for safe sex for every person in all of her/his sexual encounters and relationships. Every sexual enthusiast must calculate her/his sexual risks. Considering the possibilities of masturbation, petting, outercourse and group gropes, safe sex is limited only by your imagination. This is why the Religious Right is so obsessed with censoring your fantasies.

Also, come–ons at work are not viewed as safe sex, as the specter of sexual harassment charges can spoil the fun. Proceed with extreme tact and caution, and if you are paranoid, have the offer made through your attorney with the proper sworn affidavits, disclaimers and notarized offers of acceptance. See Safer Sex and Flirtation.

Safe Sex Travel Kit: A bag filled with condoms, lubricants with nonoxynol–9, vibrators, feathers, kneepads, massage oil, scarves, candles and matches and other essentials—including a fire extinguisher and an oxygen mask—for a spontaneous overnight stay. Some even pack latex dental dams for cunnilingus and latex gloves. What next? Latex wet suits to ensure against any bodily contacts? Get real! We're talking having sex here, not handling plutonium.

Safer Sex: This term is an unnecessary concession to prudes who cry that non–monogamous sex is never 100% safe. Neither is driving a car—which is far more dangerous than safe sex. We don't stop driving cars because of the risk of injury or death. There is no need to stop enjoying sex either. Conduct a Pre–Sex Discussion like driver's training, and use condoms and nonoxynol–9 like seat belts and airbags. Pre–testing for HIV and other STDs should be like the test you take to get your license. Then take yourselves out for a wild spin!

Saint Paul Syndrome: Based on Paul's anti–sex preaching in **The Bible**. Paul claimed, "It is good for a man not to touch a woman...It is better to marry than to burn" (Chapter Seven, First Corinthians). It may be that he had the painful burning from gonorrhea in mind at the time, but we can't be sure. Following Paul's unhealthy sexual proclamations, even marital sex was only grudgingly accepted.

Salacious: Webster must have had a fairly decent night, because at least part of his definition is sex–positive: "arousing or appealing to sexual desire or imagination." Although

Webster added "lustful," something must have annoyed him later, as he insisted that his definitions of lascivious, lecherous, obscene, indecent and lustful apply to this term. He was simply misguided. Salacious has the same root as "salivate," which is not surprising, because a salacious person often makes us salivate.

Satyr: A man who cannot be sexually satisfied due to excessive or abnormal desire. Satyrs are often depicted as having horns and lecherous smiles, but the horns are in the wrong place. Moralists use the term to apply to any man who craves sex in an effort to put him down, much as the same busybodies put down women with terms like "slut," "tramp" and "whore." See Nymphomaniac.

Scam: Getting it on as a result of scoping and scooping—the lighthearted triumvirate of terms for college students on–the–make. The student union is usually a hotbed for lusty overtures. Students enjoy browsing, looking, smelling and sometimes tasting each other in an informal atmosphere filled with laughter and pheromones.

If you "scam" someone, you connect to have sex. Note: technically you never scam—you just scammed or plan to scam. No one says "I'm scamming you now." Taken literally, the term implies an exploitive approach, but most students don't appear to take this meaning to heart very often. See Scoop, Grabbing, Scope and Score.

Scoop: While scoping out sexy people, the object is to scoop one who returns sex–on–my–mind overtures. If all goes well, you will scam (or scam with) the new tart or the campus stud. When you ask "what's the scoop?" you are probably asking for specifics as to whether magical orgasms filled the air, not what is the flavor of the day at the local dessert shop. See Scope and Scam.

Sex From Aah . . .

Scope: To check out available local talent. The term is popular among college students searching for a hot date. When students "scope out" a local dance or the Student Union, they are looking for other equally horny students for a romp on the wild side. Some students being scoped may not be equally aroused, but when the scopee is turned on with the scoper, no further distinction as to who is initiating is in order. A fifty–fifty balance of impetuous flirtation is usual during the scope ritual. Women should be assertive if they are hot for a guy. A mutual scam may be in the air. See Scoop and Scam.

Score: The goal of a sexual game where each prospective lover maneuvers for the most sublime position imaginable. Can be fun, but some are selfish and try to exploit others by leading them on with false claims of modesty, love and permanence. Also, keeping track of how many lovers you have sampled. Men often use the term as a form of bragging to indicate success in seducing ("scoring with") women, but there is no reason women cannot use the word in the same way. See Going All the Way.

Secondary Virginity: Pretending the first time never happened. If guilt didn't stop you the first time, born–agains and holy hypocrites are determined to instill fear of diseases, guilt and eternal damnation so you won't indulge in sex until you marry—if then. Someone once said he knew Doris Day before she was a virgin. See Virgin, Sexual Debut and Sex Respect.

Seeing Someone: When you don't want the person you are talking with to come on to you, you use this term as a polite but sometimes dishonest way to reject him/her: "Oh, I'm sorry, I can't go out with you because I'm *seeing* someone." Usually refers to a new sexual relationship which is more temporary than the user of the term will admit to her/himself, or to you. See Dating.

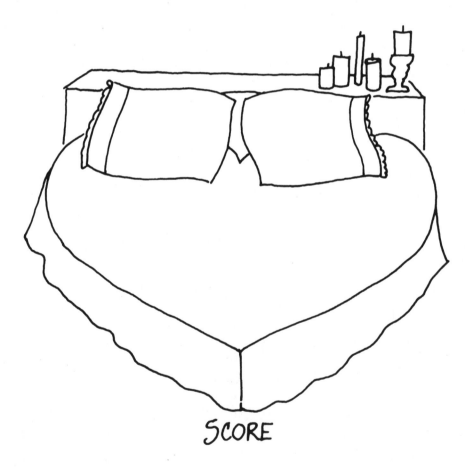

Self–Discipline: The ability to put yourself on a regular schedule to explore the garden of earthly delights without distracting interferences from work, sleep, kids, pets, in–laws or crabgrass. Sometimes it's tempting to put money or career first, but a well disciplined person will keep her/his priorities in order, and not give in to temptations less satisfying than sex. Should not be confused with self–abuse, a misnomer, which actually means the opposite...it's really self–pleasure. See Call In Well.

Semen: That wonderful white sauce that the goose may love to savor after soothing and arousing fellatio with an energized—and totally satiated—gander.

Senior Citizen Romp: A combination of aerobic exercise—including walking and visiting each other's beds (unless you sleep together) for wild sex. This is what keeps the Gray Panthers purring and pawing each other. Masters and Johnson are correct—use it or lose it. Use it a lot!

Senior Sex: Sex for older people—usually with soft massage, cuddling and changes in technique to accompany the aging process. Those over 80 can still enjoy vibrant love-making. The combined experience of the later years makes lovers extremely qualified to gyrate, dip and rise with continued vitality and a knowing smile. There's no substitute for experience, and changes in physiology, absence of interruptions by curious children and decreased need for birth control make Senior Sex one of society's best kept secrets. No wonder we call these folks WOOPIES—Well Off Older People!

Senses: Lacking with uptight people, but fully developed with sexual enthusiasts. We can utilize our senses of smell, sight, sound, taste and touch along with our intuition and our playful sense of humor! Many inhibited people lack sufficient common sense to rejoice in sex for the bountiful sensual gratification that it is. See Sensual.

Sensible: British philosopher John Wilson rightly observes that "Be sensible" is often a command to stop people from delighting in whatever they are doing— usually sex. To a moralist, to be sensible is to think about sex, but not do it! It is not sensible to avoid sex. It is sensible to conduct a proper Pre–Sex Discussion, to have both partners pre–tested for STDs and to play it safe.

Serial Monogamy: Exclusively having one lover at a time, whether for months, weeks or days. Monogamy, serial or not, can be mutually rewarding and fun. However, some need monogamy—or its illusion—to feel secure, while others are secure without feeling that a lover must only pay erotic attention to them. Serial monogamy can provide the illusion that a current lover is disease–free— a rather dangerous assumption. This is why pre–testing for STDs and safe sex need more emphasis.

700 Club: A comedy show on the Christian Broadcasting Network hosted by humorist and evangelist Pat Robertson, whose daily parody of an uptight, sexually repressed and obsessed, fanatically moralistic religious zealot is pathetically hilarious. His act often seems real, including his constant village–idiot smile and put–downs of all things sexual, pleasurable and fun. Must be seen to be believed.

In one of his funniest fund–raising letters, Robertson argued that the Equal Rights Amendment to the Iowa Constitution was part of a feminist agenda that "is about a socialist, anti–family political movement that encourages women to leave their husbands, kill their children, practice witchcraft, destroy capitalism and become lesbians." His sexual views are equally sensible and uplifting. His show is a "must" for anyone needing a good laugh.

Sex: The single most sensational pleasure known to the animal kingdom. (Sorry plants—it's just photosynthesis for you.)

SEX

Depending on whether you are mentally healthy or not, the concept may excite or scare you. Something we are not supposed to practice before marriage, even though we are expected to experience it with complete satisfaction when the time comes. Wonderfully enhanced by mutual respect and love, it is one of our greatest gifts. And yet we treat it like it is something shameful or embarrassing. Sex should be revered—not condemned! A pleasure whose value does not increase if it is "saved" for marriage.

Sexaholic: No such person exists. You can't be addicted to yourself. Sex isn't a drug. It is a real problem, however, if you unexpectedly run out of chocolate, hugs and eager lovers when all sources of supply are closed for the night.

Some members of the Sexual Addiction School of Nonsense, such as Philip Carnes, author of **Out of the Shadows,** believe that sexual enthusiasts suffer from an illness that should be treated and cured. In fact, it is SEX that should be brought out of the shadows and seen as a healthy activity to be encouraged.

The main problem with most so–called "sexaholics" or "sex addicts" is that they are not satisfied, making them frustrated and preoccupied with sex. This oxymoron term will be unheard of after the New Sexual Revolution, when orgasms will be plentiful and equally distributed.

Sex At Work: Many experts advise against this on the grounds that sex can interfere with your career, but they have it backwards—the real danger is that your work may intrude on your sex life! A fully sexual person organizes her/his life around sexual leisure rather than mundane work. Literally, having sex at work—in an office with the door locked, for example. Great fun, and a morale booster for the workers involved. See Sex Break.

Sex Between Mountains: Or between hills separated by a valley. An aroused woman holds her sensuous breasts together firmly while her lover thrusts his hard penis between them until he squirts his ejaculate. Then either or both lovers massage the fresh semen with an arousing odor and taste onto her skin. Viewed as kinky sex by those who have never tried it—usually people with an unnecessary aversion to white sauces of all kinds. An alternative to intercourse for those committed to a potpourri of safe sex practices. See Outercourse.

Sex Break: More fun than a coffee break, and more conducive to efficiency, since a relaxed and happy worker is the most productive. See Sex at Work and Quickie.

Sex Buff: A sexual enthusiast/sex fiend who relishes lust and laughter, often without clothes. A polished lover who prioritizes her/his sex life above work and other extraneous distractions. The New Sexual Revolution will usher in many more such aficionados.

Sex Contract: A written contract that says you are willing to have sex with a person. The latest in a series of contracts designed to protect some men against a charge of sexual harassment on a date. If anyone needs a contract to trust you, tell them you are due back on Planet Earth, and refer them to Geraldo Rivera. See Pleasure Pact.

Sex–Crazed: Those who prioritize sex on a daily basis. Usually involves fun–filled home deliveries. Wasn't it that "expert" on all things sexual, and every other subject, columnist Ann Landers, who wrote that if you need to have sex three times a day, you should seek professional help? This could get expensive at current street prices. Most people immersing themselves in sex this often need equally fervent lovers. See Obsession.

Sex Drive: A languishing automobile ride in the country. May include parking for awhile—a good idea for those interested in safe sex. See Libido and Autoeroticism.

Sex Education: What's missing in the curriculum. If you listen to long–winded conservative Republicans, sex education should be called "anti–sex education." Conservatives believe sex will go away if we ignore it. They are wrong. It's ironic, but most schools place much more emphasis on math than sex. We have yet to see one teenager who goes to the drive–in with a calculator and Pythagoras in mind.

Sex needs to be integrated throughout the curriculum from K–12. It is time that we have true separation of church and state. Our educators, parents and politicians should be ashamed that they are not sensible and courageous enough to promote objective and thorough sex education. We can hardly expect responsible teenagers until adults become more responsible role models.

Sex Fiend: One who celebrates "wicked good" sex as often as vasocongestion is humanly possible. It is also accurate to refer to such a person as a "sex angel" or a "sex saint," and to a repressed person as an "abstinence fiend." See Sex Maniac.

Sexist: One who puts down the other sex while asserting ill–founded superiority. It is not sexist to be sexy, or to comment on another person's sex appeal, although some extremists unfairly condemn any mention of sexiness when it applies to a woman. These same extremists love to condemn all men for the actions of a few. See Sexy.

Sex Maniac: Anyone who wants sex more than you do. A normal, healthy individual with a zest for lots of wild sex. Webster claimed such a person has an "inordinate or ungovernable enthusiasm for something." We can only wonder what Webster had in mind. Some speculate that Webster never had enough sex himself. It is unlikely that he had time for sex, although author Isaac Asimov managed to be a sex maniac in spite of writing hundreds of books.

British author Tuppy Owens updates her **Sex Maniac's Diary** annually. What a job! Her famous book is a travel guide for enthusiasts who wish to responsibly sample a variety of lovers and sexual situations. See Sex Fiend and Erotomaniac.

Sex Muscles: Our brain. Also, the PC or Pubococcygeus Muscle encompassing the lower half of the vagina and the rectum of a woman, and the base of a man's penis. We start and stop urination with this muscle. Both sexes can strengthen this muscle by contracting, holding and releasing the muscle over and over. Inhale air and squeeze the muscle for four seconds and let the air out while you relax the muscle. Repeat for five minutes twice a day, and after four to six weeks, you'll notice the difference! This facilitates more intense orgasms, and better control of arousal and orgasms— including G–Spot orgasms for women—and it helps men delay ejaculation, a boon for both sexes.

Since it is not politically correct (PC) to be a sexual enthusiast, it is *critical* that these two uses of PC not be confused! Showing a little muscle is good if it means you are a lover with good sex muscle tone. See G–Spot.

Sex Police: Our snoopy meddling government. The government has declared that your prurient interests are obscene, that any consensual partner is illegal if exchange of money is involved, and that private oral or rectal sex is punishable by fines and prison (it's true, check the books!). And some states still even have laws against nonmarital sex, including premarital sexual intercourse. The New Sexual Revolution will "Get Your Laws Off Our Bodies." See Big Brother.

Sex–With–Class: Not recommended for college professors. Being graceful and using good manners while flirting and acting on mutual fantasies. A class act is an act defined by mutual caring, sensitivity, trust and creative thrust. See Sexual Etiquette.

Sex Respect: Respecting a lover in the morning, or anytime, after consensual sex. Also, a moralistic sexual abstinence curriculum developed by right wing Bible thumpers *with a federal grant* and used in *the public schools* with a *total disregard for separation of church and state*. Sounds more like Sex Disrespect! See Secondary Virginity.

Sexologist: A specially trained and certified professional (sociologist, psychologist, medical or biological scientist) who studies and encourages healthy sexual pleasure. See Professional.

Sexual Abuse: There IS such a thing as real sexual abuse, especially when directed toward children and working women—exploitive acts which are deplorable and inexcusable. Some Catholic priests and fundamentalist preachers have become "experts" in this field. Some repressed people wrongly include normal sexual enthusiasm under the rubric of sexual addiction.

Conservative pop psychologists promote the ridiculous idea that horny people engage in compulsive behaviors because of the release of naturally arousing opiate–like hormones called endorphins. To impose any negative sexual term (such as sexual addiction) on normal, hale and hearty people is itself a serious form of sexual abuse.

Sexual Addiction: An unproven condition said by some greedy psychologists to include a non–stop obsession with sex. If this description was accurate, masturbators and other sex maniacs would never make it to work and their bills would go unpaid. Although some people are obsessive and compulsive in general, there is no logic to singling sex out as an expression of this condition.

The term was soundly rejected until the late 1980's when sexual repression became common along with the slumping economy and AIDS paranoia. Strictly speaking, addiction involves a drug or other substance foreign to the body which chemically reacts with receptors. See Sexaholic and Sexual Abuse.

Sexual Boredom: A listless feeling derived from reading most magazine articles and books about sex. A cure may be found in the use of colorful language and a more liberal philosophy. An emphasis on "just say no" and exploitive or dependent relationships quickly leads to ennui. Also, an accurate description of many long–term relationships which suffer from too much structure and routine. Those who are open and adventurous are less likely to be bored. See Sexual Variety.

Sexual Career: A sexual lifetime, or the history of an individual's sex life. Sex often stops time for hours, or at least moments. It is proper to have a sexual resumé with references available upon request. Upward, inward and outward mobility are all highly desirable. Career advancement is possible through a variety of positions held. Experience is preferred, but not required, since playful training is generally available.

May include pay (sex researcher, sex therapist, sex educator, prostitute, nude dancer, stripper, sexual surrogate and some fundamentalist clergy), or may be strictly volunteer. In either case, the activity is its own best reward. It is proper to have a sexual resumé with references available upon request. Be exquisitely graphic! See Sexual Resumé, Erotic Diary and Sexual Credit Bureau.

Sexual Compulsion: A completely normal, healthy condition, this is an overpowering need for multiple orgasms in spite of the pressures of work, children and in–laws. Some are obsessive and compulsive in their personalities, but it is unfair and inaccurate to ferret sex out from other expressions of such an imbalance. See Sexual Addiction and Sexaholic.

Sexual Credit Bureau: A modern dating service designed to quickly check out a potential lover's credentials. Previous and current lovers serve as sexual references, providing a current sexual resumé with details about a given person's likes and dislikes, as well as their noteworthy qualities and shortcomings. Personal attributes of caring, gentleness and honesty are most valuable, but outstanding technique and stamina are worthy of honorable mention. See Sexual Resumé and Erotic Agent.

Sexual Debut: A gleeful coming out (or coming–on or cuming in) party. A gain of freedom, not a loss of anything. The term connotes the first time a person experiences sexual intercourse. Some celebrate the first time with a toast. Others expect lavish coming out balls with an all nude orchestra and scantily clad waiters and cocktail waitresses. Newspapers should include photos and a brief sexual resumé to certify new entries to the sexual world.

Sexual Discrimination: An irrational bias against someone based on gender or sexual orientation. A businessman once received a 20–page questionnaire from the Federal Equal Employment Opportunity Commission stating, "List all of your employees, broken down by sex." He reported that "there are no such employees, but we do have several with drug and alcohol problems."

SEXUAL CREDIT BUREAU

Also, an unfounded bias against certain non–traditional forms of pleasure, such as gay and lesbian sex and oral sex in elevators.

Sexual Enthusiast: A perfectly normal, well–adjusted, healthy person with natural sexual inclinations and desires, who acts on them as often as possible. A bonafide sex buff who adventurously prioritizes sex above work and boring routines in her/his life. Whether monogamous or not, such a person is cheerfully into getting it on as often, and as imaginatively as is humanly possible. Some even *insist* on being strip–searched at airports!

Webster contends an enthusiast "is ardently attached to a cause, object or pursuit." He also claims enthusiasm is a "belief in special revelations of the holy spirit," and "a strong excitement of feeling, something inspiring zeal and fervor." Webster probably did not have orgasms in mind when he defined enthusiasm, but who knows? He may have been writing from a rare erotic fantasy! See Sex Maniac, Sex Buff and Sex Fiend.

Sexual Etiquette: Modern manners applied to sexual acts. Includes the sensitive reporting of fantasies along with adequate provision of towels, feathers, massage lotions, lubricants with nonoxynol–9 and condoms to assure the comfort of guest lovers. Sexual hosts and hostesses are gracious and proper in their overtures, and during lovemaking. Proper etiquette does NOT include admonitions to be abstinent, or to wait for monogamy or marriage to immerse yourself in vibrant sex. It will soon be considered rude not to invite your date to bed after an evening of fun. For women, when a man takes his clothes off, never say "Little things mean a lot." For men, this involves helping a woman come first. See Dating Etiquette.

"Excuse me, Would you pass the oil, please!"

SEXUAL ETIQUETTE

Sexual Explosion: Orgasm from escalating arousal, when you feel your soul leave your body and go to heaven. If not an out–of–body experience, certainly an out–of–pants one. In a societal sense, this will be the long overdue time when everyone opens up and lightens up about sex so we can all learn to relish it without shame. Orgasms have been around for eons. It's time that we all learn to unabashedly immerse ourselves in lots of them. See Orgasm and the New Sexual Revolution.

Sexual Freedom: A sexual right that we all deserve, regardless of our gender or our sexual orientation. Those who feel otherwise are uptight, insecure, repressed, brainwashed and just plain unhealthy. Pleasure with pride is in. Pain and shame are out. There *is* such a thing as joyous, safe and responsible sex—never mind the prudes, they will always try to limit sexual freedom— but the New Sexual Revolution is inevitable as soon as we achieve economic equality for women, victory over STDs and enhanced self–esteem. Then we all will be free to pursue pleasure without dependency, health concerns or fear of rejection. See the New Sexual Revolution.

Sexual Friend: The Fourth Option to monogamy, abstinence and promiscuity. This is a nonpossessive sexual relationship where your lover is available for thrilling trysts with you. Some sexual friendships blossom into a primary relationship, and others continue to provide lite sex for years to cum. A sexual friend is a reliable source of erotic emotion. These fuck–buddies are among our best friends, as they are not demanding or possessive, and they are always there when we need them. See Being Selective.

Sexual Hangover: An altered state of relaxation and consciousness after a night of euphoric sex, resulting in mellow satiation along with soreness and fatigue. The extended period of a warm, slightly fuzzy and delirious feeling when

SEXUAL HANGOVER

Sex From Aah . . .

all stress is gone, and you are totally wiped out. May feel like the flu for those who have experienced a literal melt–down from white–hot sex. The only known cure is more of the same with a lover who will reawaken your erotic yearning. See Afterplay.

Sexual Hangups: Something that should be checked at the door—any door—and left there. Forever. These are irrational inhibitions, such as an obsession with the missionary position (missionary zeal!), a zealous preoccupation with lifetime monogamy, or an uncontrollable need to be promiscuous. Also, hanging up on an obscene phone caller.

Sexual Harassment: Sexual aggression gone too far. Yet to be adequately defined. Sometimes wrongly confused with flirtation and sexual assertiveness—especially when a man starts it all. Even a wink, a glance or an innocent comment can lead to an harassment charge. In many cases, censorship of male sexual overtures is at stake. It is not harassing to communicate desires as long as they are reciprocated.

True sexual harassment is a very real problem. Men are the most common culprits, but it is important for women to communicate clearly when they feel men have overstepped acceptable propriety. A double standard has emerged in the workplace, where only women are permitted to flirt and to initiate playful sexual innuendo. Mutual respect and clear communication will help solve this problem.

Another rarely–discussed form of sexual harassment is the intrusion by our government, the police and religious fanatics into our consensual gratification. Both forms of harassment are equally vile and deplorable, and cannot be justified. See Flirtation, Yes, Maybe and No.

Sexual Intercourse: An open discussion about sex before and during oral and genital sexual acts. The single most sexual part of the human is the brain, so after the gray matter makes positive contact, the flesh–colored matter can do likewise. Also, penetration of a wet vagina by a hard penis in gyrating and thrusting motions common in all animals, but perfected by more highly evolved fantasy–prone humans. Our brains powerfully stimulate arousing fantasies to supercharge our motions and emotions during this cherished act. See Highly Evolved.

Sexual IQ: The amount of accurate sex information one has—and how well one uses her/his sex education. Usually measured by number and kind of mistakes—such as unwanted pregnancies and bitter ex–lovers. Positive sexual experiences rarely get enough public attention in the media, the schools and elsewhere. Otherwise, more people would have high Sexual IQ's. It is appropriate for sexual high achievers to pose as role models for others.

Sexualove: California–style. Californians rarely pause between sex and love, as both occur quickly. California sets sexual trends for the nation.

Sexual Mystery: Not knowing whom you had sex with the night before—a real "who–did–me?" Often experienced by those who had too much booze. Also, new sensations with a lover. Being open about sex doesn't make sex any less mysterious or delectable.

Sexual Olympics: Anyone who gets laid in the Bible Belt. Plans are under way to create an actual Sexual Olympic Games. The Sexual Decathlon will include muff–diving, the breaststroke, pole–vaulting (correct placement of the pole is critical), and pleasure endurance events (we are betting on the women here). The Bi–athalon will take an entirely new meaning.

Athletes will perform difficult erotic maneuvers and a medley of tantalizing positions with grace and endurance. Sexual Gymnastics and acrobatics will be featured, and Emotional Expression will also be noted in the judging of all sexual events. Tears of joy and loving embraces will be watched by millions around the world. These events give new meaning to the phrase "I'm training for Love."

Sexual Orientation: The first freshman day at liberal colleges. Also, a proclivity for one or both sexes as objects of our desire. Such a preference is the product of our genes more than our learning, although both are important. We can't choose which sex arouses us. We can only choose how to express our sexual feelings.

Sexual Preparation: This is the fore–work that precedes foreplay. For both sexes, this means first conducting a proper Libby–Morris Pre–Sex Discussion, and deciding to go ahead with sex. Also for both sexes, this means bathing, flossing, brushing, shaving and combing—all those things one does before the big prom date, but without the clothes. Then, as the two (or more) of you hit the sack, make sure you've got those bedtime essentials within reach: condoms, lubricants with nonoxynol–9, silk scarves, squirt guns and plenty of water. If you do it right, you'll laugh so hard that you'll need lots of water to quell the hiccups.

Also, men dillydallying in front of the bathroom mirror for much too long while their lovers wonder if all of a man's admiration and attention must be limited to himself. And, what a woman does in the bathroom while a man anxiously waits in bed. After brushing her teeth and putting on a sexy negligee, she drives him crazy by slowly dancing through the room without stopping to more than lightly touch or kiss him.

Sexual Problem: Whatever a sex therapist can find to justify charging $100 an hour to "solve." Since sex is defined as a problem in North America, therapists have a field day. The biggest sexual problem is not having enough sex— best solved by seeking, finding and cavorting with kindred spirits. Sex doesn't have to be a problem! But if sex is a problem, certified sex therapists are often helpful. The New Sexual Revolution will lessen the caseload of sex therapists.

Sexual Projection: New Age mental technique in which one, through concentration, projects one's spirit into the body of someone else who is being laid at that moment.

Sexual Resumé: A document which tactfully and invitingly details the sexual career of a lusty sex fiend. Should stress the positions you seek, your play experience, your special skills and dramatic highlights of your sexual career. Must include recent letters of reference from current and past lovers, and any known sexual problems or diseases. Some use perfumed paper. May be mailed or delivered in person.

Any legitimate Sexual Credit Bureau requires that all resumés be kept up–to–date. Be sure to list dates and results of recent STD tests, and any honorable mention or special awards earned while at a Petting Zoo or at the Sexual Olympics. A humorous and thorough resumé will shorten the Pre–Sex Discussion, which often leads to fun for both applicants. See Sexual Credit Bureau, Erotic Diary, Sexual Career and Hall of Fame.

Sexual Sophisticate: The cultural elite of sex. The antithesis and scourge of zany zealots who support sexual naiveté in the name of responsibility and good citizenship. To emphasize repression, New Right Republicans applaud sexual ignorance and deny sexual realities. In other words, they lie like hell in the name of "family values."

Sexual Survival: To modern day fear–mongers, the most important and difficult task for sexually active people is to survive sex in the '90's. What nonsense! You can not only survive sex, you can *immerse* yourself in it! When you find a person who is starved for affection, apply mouth–to–mouth heavy breathing. When the victim shows signs of life, move on to mouth–to–genital stimulation. The victim may require close supervision and repeated episodes of hot sex treatments if long–term survival is to be assured. Caution: With the exception of a few hospitals in Michigan, most of these essential survival techniques are still unknown! See Responsible Sex, Safe Sex and Pre–Sex Discussion.

Sexual Theme Park: With the New Sexual Revolution, erotic entertainment facilities such as "Desireland," "Desireworld" and "Orgasm Center" will emerge. Pleasure Parks will feature a "Petting Zoo," where visitors can make out with sexy "Party Animals." "Fantasy Park" will allow you to create your wildest dreams, and an "Emotional Roller–Coaster" will feature sex while experiencing dips, highs, ups, downs and other orgasmic and emotional states of being. There will be separate sections for those who enjoy romance novel settings, erotica, exotica and conventional pornography. The Dungeon and Rodeo sections will be reserved for a special few, but a Day Pass will cover it all! See Petting Zoo.

Sexuality: The intricate whole of our complex and wonderful sexual being, this is a valuable concept to be cherished, flaunted and appreciated. Should be treated as a positive and enhancing quality, rather than denied, suppressed and condemned. Sexuality is that sensational physical awareness that has resulted in the perpetuation of our species for so long. And you don't have to intend to reproduce. We already live in an overpopulated world—one more reason to emphasize nonreproductive sex!

Sexually Aggressive: A player in a power game where sex is exploitively initiated by coming on too strong. The potential lover cannot say "no thanks" or "not now" because the selfish aggressor chooses not to hear her/his protestations. See Sexual Harassment.

Sexually Assertive: Stating what you desire without imposing on others. Initiating sex through flirtation, erotic touching, kissing and related gestures of arousal and affection. The potential lover has a choice to bow out—or to bow down—gracefully. See Flirtation.

Sexy: A stunningly arousing look which causes shortness of breath, pupil dilation and genital engorgment. Accentuated by revealing clothing, tantalizing eyes and facial expressions that lead to flirtatious propositions and steamed windows. A sexy person exudes sexual desire. Also, the bait for sex. A less controversial word than sex itself, but the end result is often the same. It takes a little sex appeal to attract lovers. See Desire and Sexist.

Silk Scarves: Smooth items which can be used for amusing tie–up games where one lover controls the action while the other lover receives pure pleasure. The roles can be reversed as desired. Silk scarves are classy tools for your sexual playpen (bedroom or wherever you go to get wet and hard). Scarves are more comfortable than ropes or chains. So get a date and tie one on! See S and M.

Single: Sexually available unmarried people. Over 40% of the adult population is single. Single people deserve orgasms with each other as much as married people do. Neither group has enough of them. Both singles and marrieds suffer from gross misconceptions about each other. Singles, who spend much of their time looking for lovers, think marrieds get it all the time. Marrieds, who are often bored with monotonous monogamy, think singles have new lovers every night. While neither status is perfect, both can be satisfying. Alas, the grass is always greener—or the sex seems better—on the other side of the proverbial pleasure fence. See Available.

Single Parent: Very often, a sexually frustrated person. The demands of a job and rearing children make it hard to find time and energy for frequent sex. Those who are creative often find a way to have it all. They discuss a lover staying over with their children to be certain that the kids understand that their parent is single and has a right to a social and sexual life with selected others.

The alternative is to limit sex to quickies on the run and/or to every other weekend, when the kids are with the other parent. If kids can have friends stay over, single parents should feel free to do likewise. Why make a big deal out of it all? Sleeping over should be part of family privacy and fun. Period. See Visitation.

Singles Scene: Singles bars where ravenous people seek each other. Some are unattached, while others have primary partners, but still have a yen for an occasional new lover. Such bars are typically poorly lighted, so carry a small flashlight to discreetly check out local talent. Some seek a mate in such places, but their hot ardor is often chilled when they see their pick in the light of dawn.

Skirt Chaser: Derogatory and insulting term for a sexually zealous man, usually applied to politicians and to married men. A more accurate and positive word for such a person is "female admirer," or even "woman seeker." There is no actual female equivalent for this term, although "flirt" or "vamp" come close. You can imagine a randy woman being called a "Pants Chaser." See Manizer and Womanizer.

Sleazy: Someone below someone else's sexual standards—which may or may not be a bad place to play. One person's sleaze is another's aphrodisiac and vice versa. A dildo, for example, is an instrument of sleaze to some and the bearer of ecstasy to others. If it doesn't have disease, it may not be sleaze, so jump in and wallow around— you may be pleased with what you only thought was sleaze. For a similar moralistic term, see Promiscuous.

Sleep Around: The practice of sleeping in different beds on a regular basis. Those who do this may or may not share beds with lovers, but new beds at least provide the illusion of a new experience every night. Married people sometimes believe this wild stereotype actually describes most singles. Maybe they need to believe it to enjoy their own vicarious fantasies about what they would be like if they were single again! See Play Around.

Sleep In the Nude: A good way to keep the magic in your relationship, but it can be embarrassing on long plane trips!

Sleep With: Sleeping with another person with or without having sex. This vague and boring term sometimes implies having sex, but it is difficult to see how anyone could do this in their sleep unless simultaneous wet dreams qualify.

Sloppy Seconds: The first slurpy seconds after entry when a woman oozes natural wetness. Can lead to thrusting thirds, frothing fourths, flinging fifths and succulent sixths. Also, having sex with a woman immediately after another man. See Group Sex.

Slut: Sensuous, Liberal, Unbelievable Temptress. A naturally sexual woman who is put down for her lust for more than one lover by those having less sex than she. The term reflects the unfair bias against, and envy of, non–monogamous women who rejoice in sex for the fun of it. For centuries, men have delighted in and bragged about "conquering" women. It should come as no surprise that many modern women rejoice in "conquering" men with their irresistible sexual allure. Some wild women even wear "Slut" T–shirts cut off above a sexy navel! More power to sluts! See Tramp, Whore and Wild Woman.

Sniff Around: The practice of seeking a fellow enthusiast with one's nose. Keeping your eyes open is only part of a fine–tuned approach to new lovers. The aroma of a hot body nearby moves many to respond with escalating arousal, and it makes great scents—and good sense! See Pheromones and Scope.

Social Security: Breath mints, deodorant, condoms and other paraphernalia carried by modern lovers on a date, or during another search for adventure.

Sodomy: Oral–genital and anal sex. Illegal in several states. What kind of society are we where oral sex is illegal and masturbation is self abuse, but boxing is a sport, and hunting is wholesome unless the hunter mounts the deer?

Sourpuss: A woman who uses a dill pickle as a dildo.

Southern Belle: Lose the last "e," and you've got the major phone utility below the Mason–Dixon line. Otherwise, we're talking about those beautiful feminine creatures with long hair and lashes, hourglass figures and a propensity to use eight syllables when only three are needed. A major misconception is that these women aren't very intelligent, but don't let the accent fool you.

When properly aroused, a Southern Belle will look at you with big blue eyes, part her ruby–red lips and whisper, "Ahm as wet as the Chattahoochee River, mister, an' you bettah do somethin' about it." And then she'll proceed to guide you to her canopied bed and G–Spot...and not necessarily in that order. Southern belles typically use hand gestures and repeat key words—especially with men from other regions. When a southern belle winks and smiles, the earth shakes. See Wild Sex.

Southern Hospitality: Typified by the pervasive expression, "y'all cum!"

Space: What a lover who is losing interest asks for. Usually the beginning of the end. Also, what is found between the ears of a sex–negative fundamentalist.

Sperm: After ejaculation, at least 20 million sperm try to swim up the fallopian tubes toward a single egg—and you thought singles bars were crowded! An imagined conversation between a sperm trying to con its way past the I.U.D.: "Hey, I'm supposed to meet someone in there—I'll come right back." See Semen.

Spring: Nature's way of saying, "Let's party." That time of year when the sap begins to rise in the trees, bears and bees come out of hibernation, fish spawn and college students migrate South to celebrate sex. They spring into sex for National Orgasm Week during Spring Break every year. See National Orgasm Week.

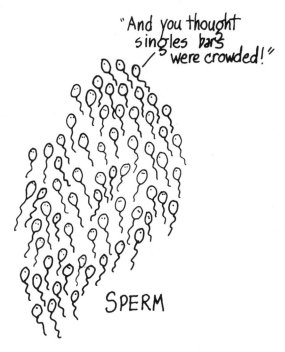

"And you thought singles bars were crowded!"

SPERM

Strok'in: As rock singer Clarence Carter suggests—stroke it to the left, stroke it to the right—just remember that strok'in is what real sex nuts do best. Strok'in is a euphemism for thrusting during fucking. Either will do, depending on your mood at the time. See Fuck and Horizontal Bop.

Stud: A desirable man who is good in bed. Such a man sometimes celebrates orgasms with more than one woman. There hasn't been a similar affirmative word for a woman who enjoys several lovers, but this is simply a Wild Woman. For an understanding of the outdated double standard, see Slut, Tramp, Whore, Promiscuous and Wild Woman.

Student Activities: Mostly sex, but also dances, parties, lectures, comedy shows and related social functions on college campuses. Coordinators of student activities have to be knowledgeable about birth control, diseases and the joys and sorrows of sexual encounters. This is because hooking up is so common on campuses across the nation. Everyone wants to hook up with someone for fun—which often includes safe sex. See Hooking Up and Condom Marshal.

Swinger: 1. One who is part of a couple that enjoys sex with others. They may meet singles or couples for sex in the same room (open swinging) or in separate areas (closed swinging). In either case, the extra–relational sex is done with the knowledge, approval and help of both members of the couple. 2. A sex buff who attends sex parties and/or advertises for lite sex lovers in sex magazines or over phone hotlines. May be married or single, but is open to more than one lover under some circumstance.

"Kinda gives new meaning to the term swinging."

SWINGING

T

Tantric Sex: Replacing movement with meditation, this is the ultimate mind–fuck. Lovers strive to come together by simultaneous breathing and fantasy, but little thrusting. Premature ejaculators beware—this sex lasts for hours! Practitioners extol this as a spiritual experience beyond the usual sexual ecstasy. In our book, focusing a meditation on sexual union beats the hell out of a mantra! See Sex Muscle.

Technological Orgasm(s): Orgasm(s) stimulated by electric vibrators such as the Hitachi Magic Wand (the Mercedes of vibrators!) or the Oster two–speed model (made by the blender company). Orgasms are almost inevitable. This is a quick way to get off—during a sex break or lunch hour, during leisure hours and when driving while aroused. It is often overlooked that men can delight in vibrators too.

It is rumored that Oster is working on a vibrator that plugs into the cigarette lighter for women on long trips. One could refer to such thrills as "blended orgasms," although the term also describes female orgasms from simultaneous clitoral and G–Spot stimulation. One can purchase an Elvis vibrator at Graceland in Memphis with three speeds: "Love me Tender," "Don't be Cruel" and "Jailhouse Rock." See Vibrator and G–Spot.

Teenage Sex: Bare beginnings of arousal and orgasms. Urgently spurred on by raging hormones in parents' homes, parked cars and isolated beaches and fields. Usually hot, sweaty, frantic, lusty—and very furtive and quick (why do you think premature ejaculation often begins during the teen years?)! Some parents fool themselves into believing that THEIR teenagers are exceptions to the rule of loving sex. Kids, if it makes them feel better, humor them! See Garment Groping, Dry Humping, Outercourse and Hot Stuff on the Couch.

Televangelist: Tell the newspapers, tell the world about these preaching boob–tube proponents of chastity. Televangelists are fundamentalist preachers who claim that sex is a sin, and that we must all ask for forgiveness for our orgasms. Such a preacher collects money—sometimes to pay for their own hypocritical indulgence in sex. See Jimmy Swaggart.

Temptation: Desire for something you want, which may or may not be a great idea. Some people can resist anything but temptation. Sometimes we're tempted by a sexy person we could have a tantalizing time with, and sometimes we just know it would spell misery for one or both. If an imminent seduction is mutual, it is tempting and definitely worth doing. However, if it is going to lead to deceit, as in the case of a married man seducing a single woman (or vice versa), trouble often is around the corner.

Trouble is what the holy hypocrites and dishonorable people usually end up with. Examples include Jimmy Swaggart and Jim Bakker. Unfortunately, evil is confused with pleasure in **The Bible's** biased treatment of this delicious concept.

Throbbing: A man when a sexy woman is in the area, and a woman when an alluring man is nearby.

Tramp: A hot woman who prioritizes sexual variety. Most women referred to as tramps or sluts are normal women who enjoy a rich diversity of lovers. A tramp is viewed by moralists as a woman who will have sex with just about anyone. But few would stoop, or lay down, to sleep with a television evangelist. Tramps are said to sleep around, but they certainly appear to be awake most of the time. They have a lot better time than "good girls." The only time a woman could rightly be called a tramp is if she's a "bum lay." See Slut, Whore and Wild Woman.

Tri–sexual: A wild soul who will virtually try anything at least three times.

Tribadism: Lesbian missionary position, where legs are locked vagina to vagina for mutual clitoral stimulation.

Tryst: Sex by appointment with a new or old lover. A new twist to an old dance. Occurs in trysting places—motels, in the woods, on a beach and at a variety of locations in apartments, dorms and homes. See Hot Stuff on the Couch.

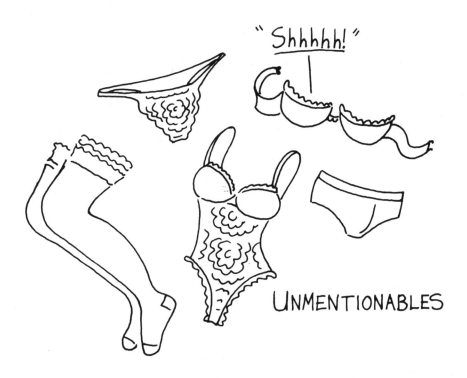

"Shhhhh!"

UNMENTIONABLES

U

USA: A repressed puritan country populated by voyeurs, couch potatoes and workaholics and a rapidly expanding group of active and healthy sex buffs.

U.F.O.'s: Unbelievably Fantastic Orgasms. Many people don't believe that these really exist. There are many reports that have been faked and fabricated. But a growing number swear to have frequently experienced such phenomena.

Unattached: A person not currently involved in a monogamous commitment to another person. Also, a couple after a sex break.

Undulate: Gentle, smooth and regular motions which stimulate the genitals during intercourse or outercourse. Such a motion is especially appropriate for the C.A.T. (Coital Alignment Technique), in which both partners control the slow rocking rhythm. The pleasure from this sensuous movement proves that we do not need to be raucous during sex in order to relish it. The quality of the experience is the ultimate measure of its delight. See Strok'in and Fuck.

Unmentionable: Usually refers to lingerie, but also includes anything positive or explicit about sex, including clothing that covers the erogenous zones. Sex fiends mention and savor that which is unmentionable to others. Polite society's hypocritical way of suppressing this explosive topic is to pretend it does not exist. See Mentionable.

Up Time: The time an erect cock teases a wet pussy while a woman hovers above her eager lover. See Down Time.

V

Vagina Envy: A feeling some men have when they wonder what it would be like to be a woman during sex. Freud failed to imagine such a condition. Men especially envy women's almost unlimited capacity for orgasmic sex, but some men experience more frequent and more intense orgasms by doing regular sex muscle exercises! See Penis Envy and Sex Muscle.

VAGINA ENVY

Valentine's Day: February 14 is a romantic holiday with little emphasis on lust or passion. Roses and flowery cards communicate love, but the original hedonistic meaning of the day was thrown out by the Christians in the middle ages—and by the Victorians in the 19th Century. A horny man who likes to have highly orgasmic sex on Valentine's Day is called a Valedicktorian. See La Festa Di Lupercalia and New Year's Eve.

Vasocongestion: The physiological cause of a wet–on and a hard–on. Extra blood accumulates in the engorged genital vessels when stimulated by arousal, titillation and erotic touch in sensitive areas. Can occur without direct stimulation during provocative fantasies and dreams. If unrelieved by orgasm, continued congestion can produce blue balls in men and pelvic aching in women. However, this usually is a delightful state leading to complete satiation, and should be savored. See Arousal.

Vatican Roulette: Of all the forms of gambling promoted or endorsed by the Catholic Church (the best known of which is bingo), Vatican Roulette has the worst odds and the greatest potential losses. It's the only form of birth control permitted by the Church—except for the "rhythm" method, or abstinence (hardly a wholesome option to being fully sexual).

Venus: The second planet from the sun, and the Greek goddess of love. Rhymes with penis—which may or may not be a coincidence—an appendage that is near and dear to every son.

Venus Butterfly Position: A popular but totally ill–defined sexual posture preceded by the Atlas Caterpillar. The name alone is erotic. The power of our imagination is captured by the mere mention of this exotic position.

Vibrator: A modern technological complement to vibrant lovemaking, vibrators usually stimulate female orgasms rapidly even if the recipient has never experienced orgasm from other sources of stimulation. This is why some college dorms have staggering electricity bills. The inventor of this handy device was inspired by a vision which came to her in a dream in which she was told: "Build it, and they will come." See Technological Orgasm(s).

Vibrating Pager: Device worn not just by women of the evening, but also by eager women and men who stick it in their pants and hope someone calls. Let your fingers do the walking!

"It's nothing we said; it's that damn vibrating pager again."

VIBRATING PAGER

Victoria's Secret: Queen Victoria's supposedly anti–sexual era was actually full of clandestine orgasms. Thus, this term. Also, a classy chain of sexy lingerie shops. More women are dressing up to go to bed, making it much harder for men to sleep all night long. See Frederick's of Hollywood.

Video Phone Sex: Gives entirely new meaning to the term, "Sexual Hangups." With video phones, you can look at the person you're turned on by. A real boon for long–distance sex, resulting in large phone bills. Warning: before undressing, make sure you don't have a wrong number! And watch out for call waiting! You may get mixed up by simultaneous conversations and fantasies, and say the right thing to the wrong person while blushing. With telephone technology advancing as it is, you may soon be able to "reach out and touch someone."

Virgin: A person who has not yet had sexual intercourse. This is natural for the young, but in adulthood such persons are rare. These days, the only thing brides lose on their honeymoon is their luggage. Sex–negative people have attempted to rescue this endangered species by uninspiring slogans and phrases such as "secondary virginity." You don't lose anything when you first have sex. Instead, you gain freedom! If you know anyone afflicted with this condition, help her/him get over it. She/he will be eternally grateful.

Some women and a few men call themselves "secondary virgins" because they try to "start over" again as a virgin. It never works! When a man asks if he was "the first," women often reply "Maybe...You look familiar. Why do all men ask the same question?" See Secondary Virginity.

Virtual Sex: Virtual ecstasy, and virtually around the corner, we hope. Virtual reality is when computers, movie film and sound are hooked up to an individual and—suddenly and miraculously—you get the sensations and feeling of whatever program is playing: race car driver, mountain climber, skydiver and downhill skier.

It's sensuround taken several degrees higher, and it's the next best thing to reality. Now imagine this new exciting technology playing programs which simulate sex. You are in a foursome of beautiful people you have selected before the virtual orgy begins. You spend the night with Cleopatra or another heroine or hero of your choice. You are at a luau with naked Tahitians. The list goes on and on...and so will the orgasms. Virtual sex is something that will definitely happen—it's only a matter of time. And another good thing: virtual sex will be much better than phone sex, while at the same time being totally safe.

Visitation: Sounds like a jail term, but this is every other weekend a divorced spouse is likely to have her/his sex life interrupted by children who are envious of any attention lavished by a lover. The other spouse has the weekend free to make up for lost sexual opportunities during the previous weekend. This is why each ex–spouse is totally wasted every other Monday morning. It makes more sense to have lovers sleep over when children are present as well as when they are with the ex. Otherwise, your home is a prison, and you are a prisoner. Such overnight visits should, of course, be done only with responsible lovers, and with careful consideration of the children's feelings (some discussion and explanation is in order). See Single Parent.

Vive La Jouissance: Leave it to the French to be sexually hot. This means "long live pleasure," or literally, "long live the pleasure to come." And pleasure ("La Plaisir") is from the female gender in French! It will be a lot easier for North Americans to be ecstatically sexual when we have more positive words for erotic delights. Three orgasmic cheers to the French!

Voluntary Abstinence: A healthy short–term choice, usually when you need to spend some time alone after a relationship breaks up. See Involuntary Abstinence.

Voyeur: One who is aroused by peeking at those who are flirting or having sex. Usually harmless to others, voyeurs often jollificate while watching the action of others. Also includes those who watch themselves and their partner during sex. Frustrated celibates and fundamentalists derive vicarious thrills from peeking at others. Sexual gourmets have mirrors on their bedroom ceilings and walls; food gourmets have mirrors on their dining room ceilings. With all the sex on television and in the movies, we are all voyeurs.

Wargasm: In America, where violence persists with accolades, it is not surprising that some get off on blood and gore. It is time to turn our sick society into a balanced society that cherishes erotic love, and which does not sanction violence or exploitation of any kind. Make love, not war. See Orgasm.

Wet–On: An aroused woman when a sexy person is in the area. A highly aroused state caused by the lustful feelings of sex–starved women. Although less visible than a man's hard–on, a wet–on can cause women to slip on the kitchen floor—or to leave a telltale stain on the couch or car seat. Women and their wetness deserve equal billing with men and their hardness. See Hard–On.

Wet Spot: The wonderful mixture of cum and vaginal juices. Some lovers agree to trade off on who sleeps on this pungent spot.

Whore: An expletive, often used as a vicious barb to put down women who play around with several lovers. Also, a woman who accepts money or other materialistic things in return for sex. May include unmarried and married women who exchange sex for security, but this is often ignored. The term more accurately describes many politicians who sell their votes, and often their souls, rather than their bodies. See Tramp, Slut and Promiscuous.

Wicked: Sex, because according to young people, it's "wicked good!" As in street argot, where "bad" means "good", "wicked"

means "great." To frothing mouths, we are said to be working for the devil. Well, we do have a hell of a good time! Sexual enthusiasts plead guilty to being brazenly wicked about sex—it's the best show in town! See Naughty.

Wicked Willie: A penis with a charming personality and a great smile. Created by British cartoonist Gray Jolliffe to add some humor to sex. See Pussy Pie.

Wild Sex: Outrageously ecstatic and spontaneous sex with some light—replaces fumbling in the dark, pointing, grunting, hallucinating and mind–reading. Uninhibited, impulsive lust without concern for work and other interferences in a lover's hedonism. Often occurs in the woods and on an isolated beach under a full moon, e.g. when you wake up at your date's apartment with her/his underpants on your head, and you can't see because your date is still in them!

Wild Thang: As in "doing the Wild Thang," fucking, pure and simple. There really is no substitute for an uninhibited, orgasmic sexual escapade.

Wild Woman: A sexy, powerful woman who frequently celebrates free flowing sexual ecstasy and is damn proud of it. Such a woman doesn't take any static from anyone. She loves to come out on top in every way. See Slut and Tramp.

W.I.M.P.: An acronym for "Woefully Intimidated Male Person," this is a man who can't stand up for himself, but who often desires to please others. Such a man often babbles during listless sex.

Womanizer: An unattached man who always carries his Safe Sex Travel Kit. A man who celebrates orgasmic pleasure with several comely women. Since there are more women than men as we age, it is confusing why such men are frowned upon. It took Ex–President Jimmy Carter to halt a heated argument about the meaning of the term between Senator Jessie Helms and Senator Ted Kennedy. Carter insisted that lust was in the heart—and that no harm could be done by a good heart. See Hustler.

Women's Liberation: In the past, this meant unhooking and burning bras. Soon this will be when women dance in the nude to drums while building their arousal for a man of their choice. Also, when women initiate sex on a date without any hesitation while sharing arousing fantasies. Requires economic liberation in the form of equal pay and opportunity, and reproductive liberation in the form of effective, shared birth control and abortion choices. See Men's Liberation.

Women's Movement: Female gyrating during sex. Also, a social movement of women concerned about social and sexual equality. See Men's Movement.

Workaholic: A sexually frustrated individual, often an American. Many Americans don't enjoy sex because they're always working or tired. A materialistic person who is more turned on by money and social status than a good lay. Ironically, many people seek money and social status so they can get laid more often. But by the time they achieve success, they're too old and tired to have fun. See Conservative Republican.

X–Rated: Arousing visual depictions of luscious sex. A sexually thrilling and explicit video or movie. Some rating boards throw in violence, but it is unclear how blood and gore qualify as thrilling—a sure sign of a society on a collision course with itself.

Y

Y–Intersection: The sensitive genital area of curvaceous women and well–toned men. We all end up there, sometimes in a traffic jam! Avoid the rush hour and proceed with caution. The green light will come. So will you! See D.W.A. and Autoeroticism.

Yes: A sex–positive word that should be used more by sexual enthusiasts when with a kindred spirit. When two people choose sex, the world is their oyster. We could use a lot more oysters. Go for a mutual yes! See No and Maybe.

Z

Zipless: No–strings–attached sex while in the nude. The "zipless fuck" was featured in Erica Jong's novel, **Fear of Flying** and in "The Woman On The Dunes", a short story by Anaïs Nin. Also, a garment that is easy to grope and remove during an erotic emergency. Finally, a penis that has lost its enthusiasm. See Zipper.

Zipper: Something that gets in the way during spontaneous lust, these multi–toothed closures are usually much faster and easier to open and close than buttons, hooks and other fasteners. (But exercise caution, especially when pulling a man's zipper up.) It's enormously arousing for partners to unzip each other and see what pops up, in or out...then in and out, in and out, etc. See Garment Groping and Fly Buttons. Also, see the sexy cover of this book!

AN AFTERWORD: TOWARD HOT SEX IN THE COOL '90's

This Glossary paves the way to a look at how we can achieve sexual liberation by balancing our sexual rights and responsibilities in **Hot Sex In the Cool '90's**, our next book. We have now established the humor and language that are necessary to discard shame and create an equal, positive approach to sexuality regardless of gender, sexual orientation and sexual lifestyle choices. The new book will argue that long term abstinence is not good for an individual's mental or physical health, and it will present a rational analysis of sexual dangers including AIDS and other sexually transmitted diseases (STDs).

Current information on AIDS is heavily biased by conservative governmental agencies and sensational media coverage. The Religious Right actually revels in fostering the anxiety and hysteria which is so characteristic of our current paranoid sexual environment. The moralistic basis of AIDS hysteria is obvious. We will show that responsible sex is safe sex. The knowledge and technology to end the spread of AIDS and other STDs is readily available and only requires a responsible and positive approach to sexual expression. A reasonable analysis of risk will also be offered, since all experts agree that the long-feared heterosexual AIDS epidemic has not materialized in this country, and few cases have occurred when neither partner is an IV drug–user, hemophiliac or a man who has had sex with men.

Hot Sex In the Cool '90's will extend the current book's basis for improved discussion between the sexes. Building on the language in this book, the second book will offer concrete suggestions to those wanting to celebrate eroticism in an exciting and mutually rewarding way. We will provide insights into how individuals can become equal partners on the same Pleasure Team, where lovers will be co-captains of the good ship "Relationship". Each relationship is the unique creation of two lovers. Using friendship and romance as a basis and sex as a key expression of love, readers are encouraged to imagine and dream together. The dreams and fantasies of both can be met if they are shared and valued in a trusting atmosphere.

The two books form a solid basis for the New Sexual Revolution. They are much of the strategy that we need to create our new revolution together. We can all become ripples which form waves of collective change toward a more humanistic, more caring and more erotic society.

We are the conspiracy. We can conspire together to create the New Sexual Revolution. We are the gentle warriors for change. We are the erotic hope for a more sexual tomorrow. We must make it clear that sex is not obscene or indecent, and it certainly as not a frill. Sex is wonderful and necessary for a balanced life.

The New Sexual Revolution will cast away all double standards, so women and those who are gay, lesbian or bisexual will be treated as total equals. To unleash our sexual love potential we must reject rigid sexual rules from religion and other sources of shame and guilt. Adding a humorous perspective makes the transition to a fully sexual and loving society more feasible.

Smoldering erotic caresses and tantalizing hands, mouths, tongues, eyes, noses and ears will complement our perpetual exploration of each other's minds, bodies and emotions. Our souls will touch and our spirits will be uplifted from genuine deepening love, lust and passion. The time to start is now!

Anyone for a Petting Zoo?!

ABOUT THE AUTHOR

Roger Libby, Ph.D., is a nationally recognized popular sex educator, sex therapist and sex researcher. A former professor at the University of Massachusetts at Amherst, Syracuse University and the University of Georgia, Dr. Libby is an invited Fellow of the Society for the Scientific Study of Sex, and an elected member of the International Academy of Sex Research. He is certified as a sex therapist by the American Board of Sexology and the American Academy of Clinical Sexologists. Dr. Libby received his Ph.D. in Sociology from Washington State University, and he completed a post-doctoral fellowship at the University of New Hampshire.

Dr. Libby is widely published, including several academic books and many journal articles. He is co-author of several articles and chapters in books with Dr. Lester Kirkendall, a sex education pioneer and co–founder of the Sex Information and Education Council of the U.S. (SIECUS), and he is co-author of the award-winning college text, **Sexual Choices**. Dr. Libby is the founder of the National Organization of Sexual Enthusiasts (NOSE) and National Orgasm Week (NOW).

Dr. Libby has been featured on numerous television programs, including The NBC Nightly News, CNN News Night, The Shirley Show on Canadian Television, Phil Donahue, Oprah Winfrey, Jenny Jones, CNBC's Real People, Montel Williams, Sally Jessy Raphael, Jerry Springer and Geraldo, among others. He has been interviewed on over five hundred radio shows, including ABC Talknet, the Mutual Broadcasting System, the American Radio Network, CBS radio and National Public Radio. His research and his insights about contemporary sexual behavior have been cited by the wire services, and by many popular magazines and newspapers, including *New Woman, Self* and *USA Today*, where he has written guest columns. He is also a co–host and a consultant for adult sex education videotapes for the Better Sex Video Series.

Originally from Seattle, Dr. Libby is single and lives in Atlanta, where he is a practicing sex therapist. Dr. Libby regularly gives humorous campus-wide presentations at universities and colleges, as well as singles groups, comedy clubs, professional conferences and other social/sexual meetings. He became a sexologist on the advice of his parents, who told him to do something he was good at!

Also by Roger Libby

Renovating Marriage: Toward New Sexual Lifestyles (co-edited with Robert Whitehurst)

Sexuality Today and Tomorrow (co-edited with Sol Gordon)

Marriage and Alternatives: Exploring Intimate Relationahips (co-edited with Robert Whitehurst)

Sexual Choices (co-authored with Gilbert Nass and Mary Pat Fisher)

To order copies of
**Sex From Aah to Zipper: A Delightful Glossary of Love,
Lust and Laughter**, by Roger Libby, Ph.D
Send $11.95 plus $3.50 Shipping and Handling to address below,
or call (404) 377-5760

*Watch for **The Pre-Sex Discussion**, coming soon!*

If you have humorous, sex–positive definitions to add
to the next edition of **Sex from Aah to Zipper**, send them to
Dr. Roger Libby at the address below. We will acknowledge
original words and definitions that we use or modify.

Speaking Engagements

Imagine Dr. Libby as a speaker for your college, singles or social group!

Dr. Roger Libby has been entertaining and enlightening college students, singles and other enthusiastic audiences around the country for many years. Have the most credentialed and the funniest speaker on sex and romantic/erotic relationships in America!

 Playful Pleasure Press ℠
& GALLERIE EROTICA
P.O. Box 8733
Atlanta, GA 30306
(404) 377-5760
FAX (404) 377-6962

Join The National Organization of Sexual Enthusiasts (NOSE)!

The National Organization of Sexual Enthusiasts (NOSE) promotes a sex–positive approach to erotic pleasure and sexual freedom with responsibility. NOSE is a political and an educational group. We support the First Amendment and our right to sexual privacy. We demand separation of church and state.

We are honest, caring and responsible in our sexual relationships. We do not support sexual license, aggressive behavior, exploitation or game-playing. It does not matter whether you are single or married, or non-monogamous or monogamous, or whether you are heterosexual, bisexual or gay or lesbian. NOSE is for all sexual enthusiasts—and for prospective enthusiasts!

We have members of all ages. Some of us are college students, others are middle-aged, and some are in their seventies and eighties!

Membership dues are $20 per year, and include a subscription to *The Sexual Enthusiast* newsletter, two bumper stickers and a membership card.

To inquire about private or public membership,
send a self-addressed stamped #10 envelope to:
NOSE, P.O. Box 8733, Atlanta, GA, 30306

Be a sexual enthusiast . . . Join NOSE Today!